Third Edition

See and Feel the Inside Move...

...the Outside

Compiled and written by
Michael Hebron, PGA MP Cl

This Third Edition of

See and Feel the Inside Move the Outside

is published in 2007 by

Learning Golf, Inc.,

495 Landing Avenue,

Smithtown, NY USA 11787

(*www.michaelhebron.com*)

ISBN: 978-0-9620214-7-3

www.michaelhebron.com

Printed in the United States of America
by Lightning Source Inc. (*www.lightningsource.com*)

Editorial assistance by Nannette Poillon McCoy for Third Edition,
Valerie Flora for First and Second Editions.

Library of Congress Control Number 2007927151

Book and cover design and layout by Martha Nichols/aMuse Productions

Golf, while not an easy game, above all is a game of ease. You are probably saying, golf may be easy for some people, but it is hard for me. I have no concentration, or I miss that ball, and I have to give it all I got or it won't ride. If there is such a thing as easy golf, there must be some formula for acquiring it. There has to be a positive method of overcoming my faults…

—Alex Morrison

Yes, there is a formula:

The Inside Moves the Outside

—Michael Hebron

PGA MP,CI

Meet the Author

MICHAEL HEBRON—*PGA Master Professional*

Michael Hebron is known and highly respected throughout the world as a creative and leading force in the professional golf instruction sector of the international golf community. Through his dedication, Michael earned the honored status of becoming the 24th "PGA of America Master Professional." This book, *See and Feel the Inside Move the Outside*, was the first golf instruction book accepted as a PGA Master's thesis. *Golf Magazine* and *Golf Digest* have consistently named Hebron as a member (since their first listings) of America's Top 50 Instructors. Over the years, Hebron has worked with many successful golfers from the PGA and LPGA tours and several national champions in America and abroad. He has also worked with many successful high school and college golfers—but Michael's pride is working with club golfers.

NATIONAL AWARDS

PGA of America **Teacher of the Year 1991**

Golf Magazine **Top 50 Instructors List 1991–present**

National PGA **Horton Smith Trophy Recipient 1990**

Top 15 *Golf Digest*'**s Teacher's Choice List** 1998–present
    (elected by peers)

Lindy Award (Junior Golf) 1973

INTERNATIONAL HONORS

Created and Coordinated:
            1990 — 1st European PGA Teaching Conference
            1989 — 1st Canadian PGA Teaching Conference
            1988 — 1st PGA of America Teaching and Coaching Summit

Consulting Instructor — Swiss PGA, French PGA, Italian PGA,
                Swedish PGA, Finland PGA

MET PGA DIVISION AWARDS

MET PGA **Horton Smith Award 1990, 1989, 1981**

MET PGA **Professional of the Year 1982**

MET PGA **Teacher of the Year 1991, 1987**

MET PGA **Honor Roll 1973**

Observations by professionals following Michael Hebron's presentation at PGA schools:

- "Keeps lessons from being boring!"
- "Great communicator!"
- "Ability to communicate is excellent!"
- "My overall reaction to his presentation: it cannot improve!"
- "Effective communicator, excellent!"
- "Gave a lot of helpful information about teaching golf!"
- "His visual aids were excellent!"
- "Super job!"

Acknowledgments

I want to express my gratitude to several people who have helped make this book possible.

First, my thanks to all the golfers I have worked with over the years. I learned from each of them. When they were pleased with their progress, it gave me the encouragement to put my approach to paper.

I am most appreciative of the PGA of America Education Department and the National Golf Foundation for the opportunity to give clinics and workshops all over the world. Those assignments helped develop and test my ideas.

My thanks to my fellow PGA golf professionals, who took an interest and helped me grow as a person and a professional, and to "G.B.G.B."

The membership at my club, Smithtown Landing Country Club on Long Island, has always played a part in any progress I have made in golf, including this book.

Lastly, I thank my friends and family—a very special thanks to both for their support over the years.

Michael Hebron

Table of Contents

Foreword

Believe it or not:

- Physical talent is important in any sport, but it is truly insignificant when compared to the mental aspect of learning.
- The backswing is only a few inches long.
- Poor shots or swings happen only when rotational forces stop or are interrupted.
- To have a late release, to retain the angle, or to hit late, golfers with sound swings do nothing with their hands and arms.
- The *what-to* in golf is important but the **feel** of *what-to* is also important.
- Our nervous system is more important than our muscle system.
- Balance is a result of a low center of gravity and counterbalance.

We are often misled by the types of information stored in the mind's eye:

- Without question, the most important keys in golf are the *concepts* and *visualizations* of the swing that are stored in your mind's eye.
- The golf swing that your body will try to make is based on the concepts and visualizations you have in your mind's eye.
- We can be misled in golf by what we *thought* we saw and felt.
- We must learn to recognize the difference between a golfer's personal mannerisms and the actions and movements of a sound swing.
- Understanding core knowledge leads to a sound swing.
- The body does *not* move on its own—movement happens for one of three reasons: reflexes, anticipation, or the muscles receiving a command message from the mind.
- Your mind does not hit the ball, but it can stop the swing.

- We must change on the *inside* first, and then work on the outside.
- We must learn how to train the mind.

As I look back on those early days, I suppose that in my youthful mind, I was dimly aware that the quality of my game was going to be forever tied to the elements of sacrifice and personal discipline. Success is closely tied to determination, and that quality is not precisely related to native talent. I was a poor player and slow in attaining my goals; a late maturer, they call it.

—Ben Hogan

Third Edition Introduction

Welcome to the third edition of *See and Feel the Inside Move the Outside*. The first edition was published in 1984. Those 500 copies were followed later that year by an expanded second edition. Twenty years later, more than 25,000 copies have been purchased, and there are still several requests a week for this book.

To be honest, I was surprised by the interest the golf community showed in this book based on notes I had made from the early 1970s to the mid-1980s about learning to play golf.

I did not write *See and Feel the Inside Move the Outside* as a "how-to-play-golf" book. It was compiled from a variety of valuable sources in the hope that it would provide readers with insights and points of view for playing golf with an efficient golf swing. This third edition is influenced more by research into the nature of learning than the first and second editions were. *Note*: Any attempt to share information becomes more efficient when it takes into consideration the nature of learning or how one actually goes from not knowing to knowing and how lessons provided become lessons learned.

The information in *See and Feel the Inside Move the Outside* is a description of what has happened (and I stress what *has happened*) during an efficient golf swing that has golfers' large muscles moving their small muscles—what I refer to as the *inside* moving the *outside*.

The ideas and information in this book are not intended to be a blueprint for *how* to swing. They are meant to help create insights about *what-to-do* through feels and images that are personal in nature. I have found that the *personal* acts of *how-to* arrive through the trial and feedback of swinging, observing the outcome, then making adjustments if needed—based on past experiences and core golf knowledge.

One example of a what-to-do suggestion is "Swing the club shaft *through* impact before the clubface." Studies into the nature of learning show that a what-to-do concept is more useful than focusing on *how-to* directions. This holds true especially if the *how-to* directions are coming from a source other than your own personal self-discovery. The general requirements of a particular event, or its *core knowledge*, can come from a source beyond the performer—for example, shaft before clubface or shoot the basketball *up*—but studies show that receiving and focusing on detailed instruction about *how* to do something can fragment progress.

Speaking of core knowledge, the elements that make up the short list of golf's core knowledge also make up the list of things to do. Golfers should

- Swing the weight of the club.
- Swing the weight of the club with a rhythm and balance that can be repeated.
- Swing the club with no emotional attachment to results.
- Swing the club based on a model that the shot you are about to play provides.
- Swing the shaft of the club through impact before the clubface with the shaft swinging *parallel* to the angle it occupied at address.
- Swing the weight of the club with the large muscles of the body helping to swing the small muscles of the body and the club.

In my view, the most efficient approach for learning to apply golf's core knowledge is through self-discovery in a learning environment free of detailed directions and corrections from sources beyond the self-discovering golfer. Sound studies into the nature of learning support this approach to progress based on self-assessment and self-development..

There are only a few possibilities concerning the golf swing:

1. **Clubs are either swinging through impact on a plane that's too high, too low, or just right for the shot being played.**
2. **The club's head and face are either behind or in front of the left wrist through impact.**
3. **Clubs are either swinging in rhythm or they are not.**

In my view, that is all there is.

I have found that it is useful to focus on the positive thought of what to do with the golf club and not on trying to fix poor outcomes. Studies have shown that trying to fix something does not lead to learning that lasts—but focusing on what-to-do *does* lead to learning that lasts. Again, I would suggest that golf's core knowledge provides insight into what to do with a golf club. The design of a golf club and the requirements of the shot a golfer is about to play dictate what the golf swing should do with the club.

Other Titles by Michael Hebron

Blueprints for Building Your Golf Swing (DVD and Video)

Art & Zen of Learning Golf

Building & Improving Your Golf Mind, Golf Body, Golf Swing

Building & Improving Your Golf Mind

Building & Improving Your Golf Body

Building & Improving Your Golf Swing

Golf Swing Secrets…and Lies

Golf Mind, Golf Body, Golf Swing — DVD Set

Blueprints for Parents and Children Learning Golf —
DVD with French translation feature

Part 1

Your Mind's Eye

I have always believed that if golfers could see a sound golf swing clearly in their mind's eye before they tried to take a swing, this would be useful for improving that golfer's own game.

> **Ben Hogan** told us, "The average golfer's problem is not so much the lack of ability, as it is a lack of knowledge about what he should be doing." When you can mentally picture what you are trying to do, or are being asked to do, the task is more than half done. With an understanding of your swing in your mind's eye, future lessons can be more helpful. In fact, the improvement can be dramatic! This is not only true in golf but in any endeavor. I hope the information that this book gives you a clear understanding of what you would like to do with when making your swing.

Bobby Jones talked in depth about the mind. "The one influence most likely to assure the satisfactory progression of the swing is clear visualization in the player's mind of movements. This can do more for a player than anything else he can possibly do, and I stress this point."

Jack Nicklaus felt that "Many golfers probably do not understand cause-and-effect factors."

Alex Morrison, the most respected teacher of his time, wrote, "The excellence of your game will depend upon the extent to which your mind takes charge, and the way your body responds to its commands." Alex's book, *Better Golf Without Practice*, was devoted to the use of "the mind's eye." The book was a top seller and considered a masterpiece. While reflexes and anticipation are the tools needed in other sports, the main tools of playing successful golf are *visualization* and *conceptions*. They are the two most important aids for playing successful golf.

It is the ability to use our reflexes and anticipation skills that makes our performances better in most sports—for example, to anticipate correctly where an opponent will hit the tennis ball, to anticipate where the ball is about to be passed in basketball, to anticipate the kind of pitch about to be delivered, to anticipate the next play the quarterback will call…I could go on…but this does not always hold true for golf. In golf, our ability to make a sound swing is based on visualization and conceptions: It is how you "see" the movements you would like to make with your golf club—before you step up to the ball—that can make the difference in your game, whether it involves a putt, a greenside chip, or a tee shot.

Good golfers have a clearer visualization of what they want to do with their club before they swing. They also remember the feel of the swing, good or bad. Our bodies do not move on their own. Movement comes from one of three reasons: reflexes, anticipation, or the muscles receiving a mental command message.

It is a mental message sent through the nervous system that is responsible for the actions and movements that make up the golf swing. The basketball foul shot and the bowling motion work the same way: As these two athletic movements start, the mind tells the body what to do. In golf, there is no opponent causing movement. Instead, *we create the swing* based on the conditions for the current shot. The opponent's actions do not cause the movements. The movements are a self-imposed creation, not a reaction or movement of anticipation.

Keep in mind that the message sent is based on the information stored in our mind. If you have poor concepts and visualizations, your swing is performing under that handicap. When looking at the swings many golfers make, it seems fair to assume that those golfers do not have the kind of worthwhile concepts and visualizations that they should have.

I made some notes while having breakfast with the well-known golf coach Chuck Hogan, the author of *Five Days to Golfing Excellence* (a book every serious golfer should own). Chuck was familiar with my work, and I knew of his success in working on the mental side of the game of tour players, including Peter Jacobsen, Johnny Miller, Mary Beth Zimmerman, and Barbara Mizrahie. Our breakfast turned into a wonderful three-hour exchange of ideas. Here are a few of my notes from that time spent with Chuck in 1983:

Golf Is a Creative Process . . .

Your understanding of the swing is what makes the proper swing. The proper swing does not create understanding.

You can create only after gathering information about a situation, reflecting on it, and then reacting to it.

You can respond efficiently only when you remain receptive to information being provided by the target. If you shift your attention to yourself, you remove your attention from the target.

Example: You should address the putt, look at the target, and then make your swing. Telling yourself you have not made a putt all day as you stand over your next putt is not the correct approach.

Golf is both mental and physical. The body only does what the brain commands. The eyes do not see; the ears do not hear; the mouth does not taste; the fingers do not feel; the nose does not smell. These body parts are merely receptors for brain information. It's the brain that deciphers all the information provided by the sensory organs.

Humans are biocomputers of sorts—the brain is the computer processor, the body is the print-out, and images are the software program. Your body—and subsequently your golf club—will do what the software (images) commands it to do. Body movements are always efficient. The body will only do what it has been told to do by the brain. When your swing produces a shot you are not happy with, please realize your brain produced that swing! The swing did not just happen, your body efficiently responded to the message your brain sent out.

"It is not the golf swing that is responsible for a poor shot; it is one's state of mind that created that particular golf swing!" (Susan Berdoy Meyers)

In my view, the most important keys in golf are the useful concepts and visualizations of the swing that are stored in the mind's eye. After you *have* useful concepts and visualizations, they must be put to use from a stance or posture that is useful and does not lose its balance during the swing. A sound swing is being influenced by the laws of motion; a change in the balance of a golfer's posture during a swing would interrupt that influence. A change in balance during the swing may cause the angle of the spine to move, the center of gravity to change, or the base of support to be altered (to mention only a few possibilities). Any of these changes will destroy an otherwise sound swing by altering the plane or path of the club head. A useful setup that is *not* altered during the swing should be the goal of every golfer: spine is tilted over to the ball, head or chin is up off the chest, the knees are flexed, and the buttocks are out.

How Learning with the Mind's Eye Works

Think of your brain as a *split brain*. It is made up of a left hemisphere and a right hemisphere, each with separate responsibilities when the brain is working correctly. The California Institute of Technology is a leader in providing facts and information on the endless workings of the brain, and some of their research follows.

The *left hemisphere* works with *verbal* information, while the *right hemisphere* works with *visual* information.

They are two separate forms of information—they are *not* alike. I suggest that we must learn to see the sound golf swing without being misled by what we are looking at. You have heard some good players say that they do not think (left side: verbal) about their swing when playing. Also, some fine instructors will state that it is possible to think (left side: verbal) too much when playing. I strongly agree with both statements.

But no one has ever suggested *not* to picture (right side: visual), feel, or visualize beforehand what you would like to do when playing golf. What I suggest to my students is to stop playing golf using words—up, down, fast, in, out (left side: verbal)—and start to rely on concepts, pictures, feels, and visualizations, which are all right-side (visual) functions. This approach has been very successful with students at all levels.

Learning to improve your golf game involves more than learning the physical skill. Learning to use the brain's right hemisphere will lead to lasting improvements—to see and to feel a sound golf swing is the goal.

In the realm of artists and painters, it is said that the great ones can see more than average artists. They learn how to really *see*. "The painter draws with his eyes, not with his hands. Whatever he sees, if he sees it clear, he can put down." (Maurice Grosser)

"Learning to draw is really a matter of learning to see, to see correctly—and that means a good deal more than merely looking with the eyes." (Kimon Nicolaides)

Betty Edwards tells us, "Artists say that they feel alert and aware yet are relaxed and free of anxiety, experiencing a pleasurable, almost mystical, activation of the mind." I think most golfers would like to be in this state of mind when playing.

In my approach to helping individuals learn golf, I tell my students that a round of golf is not *one* game but 70, 80, or 90 separate times the mind is *subconsciously* telling the body what to do; 70, 80, or 90 separate performances; 70, 80, or 90 separate pictures to be mentally drawn. The game of golf is played by creating golf swings, and the better or more clearly you can see that swing before you try to perform it, the better your chances are for success. Most of the education we have been exposed to over the years has been geared to words and the left hemisphere—the analytical. In fact, it has been discovered that the left hemisphere will take over the thinking process in most circumstances. I hope this book will help you use and learn to trust your *right* hemisphere more often than the naturally dominant left hemisphere. Keep in mind that the thinking process happens in two modes—words and pictures. I suggest you learn to play golf by using mental pictures and not verbal suggestions that cannot be turned into a subconscious visualization.

> You should not concentrate, if it is taken to mean such a pulling of oneself together, such a fixing of the mind on the task at hand, such a tight-lipped determination to do one's best, that golf becomes a trial of nervous strength rather than a game. I say that a golfer can only produce his true quality when he can play without concentrating (in a sense), when he can make his shots without clenching his teeth.... The good golfer feels his swing as all one piece. It is produced by a psychophysical unison and its control is outside the mind of the player. Any control that is within the mind is subject to the state of the mind and is therefore unreliable. ... Good golf, consistent golf, depends upon being able to shut out our mental machinery (with its knowledge of the difficulties of the shot, the state of the game, etc.) from those parts of us that play golf shots.
>
> —Percy Boomer

For me to be of any help as a teacher, I must know what a student is trying to do when making his or her swing. When I meet with someone for the first time, this is a *must-ask* question for me to ask, because it is the starting point for a coach and student.

We have all heard "What you believe *isn't* always what you get." Contemplate this: A golfer may describe a swing that in execution becomes a very different swing from the one he just described. The way they actually swing is not what they perceive their swing to be (i.e., saying one thing and doing something else). Then, too, after hearing students tell me what they think the swing "should" be or what they are "trying" to do, I often find they are misinformed about the golf swing, and therefore they do not have a worthwhile approach. If you were to write about your swing, I believe it would help you more than you may think!

Someone suggested that I write about my own swing very early in my professional career, and it proved to be most helpful.

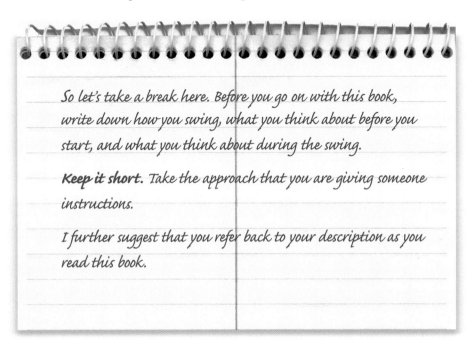

So let's take a break here. Before you go on with this book, write down how you swing, what you think about before you start, and what you think about during the swing.

Keep it short. Take the approach that you are giving someone instructions.

I further suggest that you refer back to your description as you read this book.

The Two Modes of Information Processing

Inside each human head there is a double brain with two ways of knowing.

The brain's left hemisphere analyzes, abstracts, counts, marks time, plans step-by-step procedures, verbalizes, and makes rational statements based on logic. For example, given variables a, b, and c, we can say that if a is greater than b and b is greater than c, then a is necessarily greater than c. This statement illustrates the brain's left-hemisphere mode: the analytic, verbal, figuring-out, sequential, symbolic, linear, objective mode.

On the other hand, we have another way of knowing: the brain's right hemisphere mode. Some of the things we see in this mode may be imaginary. We see how things exist in space and how the parts go together to make up the whole. Using the brain's right hemisphere, we understand metaphors, we dream, and we create new combinations of ideas. When something is too complex to describe, we can make gestures that communicate. Psychologist David Galin has a favorite example: Try to describe a spiral staircase without making a spiral gesture. Using the brain's right hemisphere, we are able to draw pictures of our perceptions. A general image of a golf swing is more useful for learning than using a detailed description.

In a speech given in Snowmass, Colorado, in 1977, Dr. J. William Bergquist, a mathematician and specialist in the computer language known as APL, proposed that we can look forward to computers that combine digital and analog functions in one machine. Dr. Bergquist dubbed his machine "The Bifurcated Computer." He claimed that such a computer would function similarly to the two halves of the human brain.

Jerry Levy (**Psychobiological Implications of Bilateral Asymmetry**) said, "The left hemisphere analyzes over time, whereas the right hemisphere synthesizes over space." As processing technology moves forward at an ever increasing speed, this comment reminds me of the to the 2005 dual core processors, each taking different parts of a task to produce the results at a much faster speed than in the past.

We Can Be Misled by What We Think We See and Feel

When video replay became available, we in professional golf were looking forward to the very real prospect of being able to help golfers get more out of their game by reshowing a swing only seconds after it was made. How wondrous—surely this new tool would be a breakthrough for both the student and the teacher, but new research has lowered these expectations.

At that time, it was my belief (and that of other golf professionals) that golfers could be helped by this new teaching aid. I am sure that most golfers felt their swing had to be improved and believed video replay might improve their visualization. At this writing, a decade and a half later, there is still a real lack of understanding of how video replay can actually *impede* the progress that golfers look for. Why do I say it can *hinder* progress? Because it is *negative reinforcement*. Showing someone what they do wrong does not enhance learning. Studies show that video replay is not as useful as we once thought it would be. There are some exceptions, but I now use mirrors more often than video.

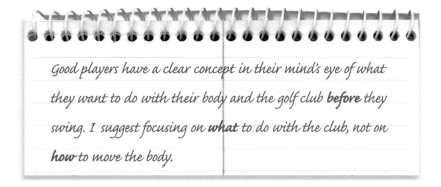

> *Good players have a clear concept in their mind's eye of what they want to do with their body and the golf club **before** they swing. I suggest focusing on **what** to do with the club, not on **how** to move the body.*

One example of being misled is the length of the backswing. I have asked students of all abilities to put the club at the spot they feel or think it reaches at the top or end of their backswing. Few have ever put the club at their top spot—very few, in all the years I have been teaching! After most are shown where their club actually travels to, it is met with disbelief: "I don't believe it!" or "You have to be kidding!"

This clearly illustrates how easy it is to be fooled by what you *think* you are doing! The golfers' *feel* has misled them. Most take the club back farther than they think they do.

> Alex Morrison told this story about Bobby Jones: "When Jones first saw slow-motion pictures of his swing, he was astounded to note that the details of his golf swing differed markedly from the golf swing he believed he was making. Bob would occasionally make statements regarding the execution of shots that were not consistent with what was actually taking place." Morrison went on, "I have motion pictures of Jones and other great players which show conclusively that their own ideas of the swing and the actual swing they make are at wide variance."

To be misled by what you think you are *seeing* is also very common. Most golfers are not aimed where they think they are. Also, when looking at a fine player's swing, you can be tricked. Seeing the club head move at 100 mph or more creating a lot of power and with the ball going considerable distance, the onlooker may think they are seeing a lot of effort at work. This is not true; they have been misled.

I have listed only a few examples of misconceptions, and if your mind's eye uses *mis*conceptions as *con*cepts (or visualizations) on which you base your swing and game, playing golf will be much harder than it should be.

I am going to give you some different ways of looking at the golf swing. These concepts and visualizations can be the foundation for the progress you are capable of—and have been looking for. I feel there will be an understanding of the swing that you have not had before. It will become easier to have a picture in your mind's eye of what you would like to do with your club before making the swing.

Learning about feel can also help with your visualization and concepts. In 1980, I sent a questionnaire to the men and women who play their respective PGA and LPGA tours, various outstanding amateurs, and several club professionals who play tournament golf. Having friends in all those categories, I expected a good response, and I was not disappointed. What I wanted was to gather information about what good players *feel* when they play and not *how* they play. What did they feel when they held the club? What did they feel at address? What did the backswing and the downswing feel like? At the end of the swing, was there any special feel? What about the head? I also asked if they had any personal thoughts about the subject of *feel* (*see Survey section*).

I asked only a few questions but received a lot of useful information. Golfers with a sound swing, low handicappers, and professionals all remember the feel of their swing. They have taught themselves to repeat that feel (or touch) the next time they have the same type of shot. You have heard this incorrectly referred to as *muscle memory*. Memory is in the brain, not the muscle.

Golfers should not go over a specific "how-to" list on the golf course. Before the swing takes place, visualizations and feel (both in the brain) can help golfers prepare for the swing. If the swing is going to be repeated, you must remember what the swing feels like to you. Whether you make a good or bad swing, the *individual characteristics* of what you feel as you swing the club must be remembered and recognized: fast, slow, short, long, up, down, etc. Everyone will feel his or her own swing a little differently, and it is this individual *feel* that is going to help you, perhaps more than you can believe.

Learning is natural, and learning is fun—or it should be. If you think you can learn, there is a good chance you will! If your goal is to have a swing that can respond to "muscle memory," please accept that you should not be trying to memorize a lot of *how-to* directions. Progress *is* on the way when the feel of the swing (what to do with the golf club) becomes more important than *how-to* directions. We will spend more time on the subject of feel later, so for now, let's review:

- Progress will come *only* if you make the effort in a safe learning environment.
- Progress is based (in part) on self-discovery; not on teaching—fixing environments.
- Suggestions you work with *must be* worthwhile.
- The body does not move on its own—*reflexes, anticipation,* and *mental messages* create movement.
- Define the difference between personal mannerisms of a golfer and the movements and actions that exist in all sound swings.
- *Concepts* and *visualizations* stored in your mind's eye are the most important keys in golf!
- We can be misled in golf by what we see.

- Feel must become more important than thinking about *how-to* directions.
- The right hemisphere of the brain can be more helpful than the left hemisphere.

Understanding and Seeing Angular Momentum, Rotational Forces, and Inertia at Work

An observation that most if not all golf professionals would agree on is that "A sound golf swing possesses inertia, angular momentum, and rotational forces."

Rotational force, or center force, is the principle of force (or power) that is directed or created from a central point. It is a developing force, moving from the center outward.

Inertia is defined as matter that, if kept moving, will stay on the same path unless affected by an outside force.

Good golf shots are a result of a sound swing that has rotational force. Conversely, bad golf shots or swings occur when there is no rotational force or when centrifugal force is interrupted or stopped. Look at a sound swing or any efficient athletic movement and you are seeing rotational forces, inertia, and angular momentum at work.

Power in golf and other sports comes from rotational forces, and how athletes visualize those forces at work within the movements of the body during those sports is important. Visualizing those forces correctly is one key to progress, so let's spend some time on the subject.

The expression we are going to use in explaining rotational force is *The Inside Moves the Outside*. Keep in mind the following key words from the definition of rotational forces:

- inner point
- central point

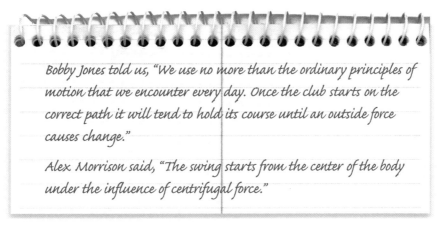

> *Bobby Jones told us, "We use no more than the ordinary principles of motion that we encounter every day. Once the club starts on the correct path it will tend to hold its course until an outside force causes change."*
>
> *Alex Morrison said, "The swing starts from the center of the body under the influence of centrifugal force."*

- developing
- moves outward
- keep moving
- outside force

Remember:
- Power and energy from rotational forces are *developing forces*—forces that build up.
- Power and energy from rotational forces move outward from an inner or central point.
- Inertia will keep matter moving in the same direction unless affected by outside forces.

I am spending time with an explanation of rotational forces so that when I use this terminology later, your mind's eye will have a worthwhile and clear concept of how a sound golf swing is under the influence of rotational forces when the *inside is moving the outside*.

Angular momentum is the final factor to understanding the workings of a sound golf swing. Angular momentum, or the rotation of a mass around an axis, is in a subdivision of physics called *mechanics*. When an object rotates around a fixed axis, it will rotate at a constant rate of speed (until friction or gravity slows it down) as long as the object's total mass stays the same distance from the axis when rotating. When the object's mass is brought closer to the axis, it automatically speeds up, and if part of the object mass is moved further out from the axis, the object slows down. An example of this is the ice skater who is spinning at the center of the ice: the closer the arms of the skater are moved to the center—or axis—

of the body mass, the faster the skater will spin. The farther away the arms are moved from the skater's axis, the slower the spin becomes. The laws of motion and physics explain this result by stating that if the distribution of mass (or weight) with respect to the axis or center of the mass is changed, the rotational speed will change.

Science also tell us that the momentum or speed created by rotation will generally move to the part of the system with the lesser mass—in other words, to the part that is easiest to move. When a long whip is snapped, the momentum travels away from the body mass to the arm, to the hand, into the handle of the whip, and out to the tip end of the whip. This tip has the least mass and therefore is the easiest place for the momentum and speed to go. The tip end, in fact, travels so fast that when the whip cracks, the tip is moving several hundred miles per hour.

When these three laws of physics—angular momentum, rotational forces, and inertia—are present in the golf swing, a golfer does not have to apply any conscious effort with his hands, arms, or club to produce a swing—it happens because of these laws of motion.

Angular momentum, rotational forces, and inertia have each been explained separately. Now let's see how they work with each other as a team. When mass resists a change in its motion, it has what is called *inertia*. Inertia can keep a mass moving in a straight line until affected by an outside force. The mass is also picking up velocity. *If the action that puts a mass in motion is circular or rotary, rotational forces will soon be present and stay present as long as the circular motion exists.*

Keep in mind that inertia wants to keep matter moving in a line. At the same time, the circular or rotary system is trying to move the mass in an arc. Due to the fact that these two forces are working against each other, centrifugal force is born, causing the bottom of the golf club shaft and the club head to bend downward during impact. As the hub, or center part, of the system is turning in a circle, the outer part that is trying to go in a straight line starts to pull against the hub. This pull is called *rotational force*, and it is what athletes feel when they are in motion. Rotational force is an outside force that interrupts inertia and causes the outer part of the system to follow the lead of the hub and move in an arc or circle instead of the straight line demanded by inertia.

Also, momentum and speed have traveled out to the tip end of the system because of angular momentum. A sound golf swing moves in an arc. As you read on, I hope you gain an understanding of these two descriptions of the swing. When the quality of the swing is lower than we would like, it is because rotational force has been interrupted or stopped, and the swing stops moving in an arc.

Now, it's time to talk about the *inside moving the outside*. Visualize a yardstick or put one down on a table. Now put your hand on the stick at the 3-inch mark. Put your hand on the bottom of the stick. Now move the top of the stick left or right a few inches. Note how much more the top part of the top of the stick moves (*outside*) than the bottom of the stick (*inside*). When the *inside is moving the outside*, the *outside* is moved a much greater distance. This fact of math will relate to your golf swing concepts shortly.

A related math and physics concept that will help you to understand your golf swing is that when the *inside* moves slowly, the *outside* is moved much faster! Visualize a skate line in an ice show. You can see that the 20 to 30 skaters standing shoulder-to-shoulder start to move in a big circle. In a short time, the *outside* skater is being moved at a great speed and distance, while the *inside* skater is moving a very short distance and at a much slower speed. All the *outside* skater has to do is hold on. The *outside* skater could not move any faster or have more power if she tried to skate on her own. In fact, if the *outside* skater were to let go of the line and try to duplicate the speed and power that existed while she was still holding on, we know it could not be done.

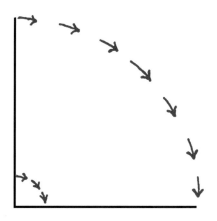

The inside moving the outside is leverage, wherein a small inside displacement causes a large outside displacement.

Here is another example: When a door closes, the inside of the door moves only inches and moves slowly, while the outside of the door moves many feet at a faster pace.

With these visualizations in your mind's eye, you can start to build a sound swing. These are easily recognized examples of the *inside moving the outside* that answer questions about what makes a sound swing work.

The Inside Moves the Outside

In golf instruction, we ask people to label the arms, hands, and club—or whatever is being held—as the *outside*, and the rest of the body, feet, legs, hips, chest, shoulders, and head as the *inside*.

When making a golf swing, I want people to have their *inside moving their outside*. To put it another way, I do not want golfers to use their arms consciously during the swing. It seems that when the arms are used, rotational force is either stopped or interrupted. When you consciously do nothing with the arms, they will follow the laws of physics and perform as they should in a sound swing. Energy in golf or other sports is a result of a transfer of weight; you cannot transfer weight just with your hands and arms (a.k.a. *the outside*)! Weight will be rotated back and forth by your body (a.k.a. *the inside*).

When asking you to see that the *inside moves the outside* in sports, I am also talking about the transfer of weight that is part of every efficient athletic movement that is under the influence of rotational forces. Your golf swing is very personal to you. At times it is very hard to get golfers to change their minds about what they should be trying to do with their swings. My hope for you is improvement. I believe that the arms do not have to do anything consciously in a sound golf swing. With the visualizations and concepts that will be shared with you, along with the statements from some very knowledgeable individuals, you may start to feel that the *inside moves the outside*.

"Golf, while not an easy game, above all is a game of ease," Alex Morrison told us; he went on, "You are probably saying, golf may be easy for you or some people, but it is hard for me. I have to concentrate or I'll miss the ball and I have to give it all I got or it won't ride. If there is such a thing as easy golf, there must be some formula for acquiring it. There has to be a positive method of overcoming my faults."

There is a formula: *The inside moves the outside!* Listed below are a few of the many statements I have come across over the years suggesting the same approach to the swing.

Tom Watson, Jack Nicklaus, and Alex Morrison talked at length about the hands and arms playing a less important role in the swing than they had originally visualized.

Alex told us, "I have been convinced. A careful study of the technique of every expert who has played in the United States proves conclusively that every successful shot played by any one of them is the direct result of the employment of centrifugal force. Despite everything I had heard I could not make myself believe that the main force of a golf swing should originate in the hands and arms. Trial and experiment demonstrated to me that the necessary whirling motion of the club was produced only when the force activating the club had its origin near the center of the body."

"Moreover, Bobby Jones' swing illustrates this motion better than the swing of any other golfer. In other words, the sound golf swing is not my swing, nor Jones's, nor Smith's, but simply the exemplification of a scientific principle correctly applied. My definition of the swing is 'One full smooth flowing motion without any mental or physical interruption.' Only by winding up the body to its fullest, then releasing the accumulated force in any expanding motion, can a golf club be swung easily, naturally, accurately, and with maximum power."

Jack Nicklaus, since the spring of 1980, has changed his beliefs about the golf swing. His highflying arms always marked his swing. He now feels some of what he wrote or said in clinics in the past is incorrect and contrary to how he tries to swing today. (He had lost power with his old swing.) Jack, knowing that playing golf is always a learning process, said with apologies, "I decided to find a new and better golf swing. If the arms are overextended early in the backswing, it is a lazy, lift up, chop way to play—extremely common among recreational golfers. My challenge was to flatten my swing, so I began hugging the upper chest with my arms in the backswing."

Ben Hogan: "The action of the arms is motivated by the movements of the body, and the hands consciously do nothing but maintain a firm grip on the club."

Bobby Jones: "The proper order of movement is body, then arms, and last the club head."

Alex Morrison: The swing starts from the center of the body, under the influence of centrifugal force."

Paul Runyan: "The swing is entirely controlled by the shifting and turning of body weight. The arms become a connecting link, and nothing more, between the pivot point and the club head."

Ben Hogan: "The main thing for the average golfer is to keep any conscious hand action out of his swing. The correct swing is founded on a chain action. If you use the hands when you should not, you prevent the chain action."

Paul Runyan: "It is my experience that as you 'cease' consciously directing the swing by the use of shoulders and arm muscles, you establish an automatic grooved swing."

Carl Lohren: "Whenever the arms and hands are involved in your mental concept, they will steal the show. If the hands and arms move first, they will not direct the club in the proper direction."

Ben Hogan: "Next time you see a good player in action; note how his body appears to drive forward before he hits the ball."

Paul Runyan: "Do not try to uncock or snap your wrists. This is an automatic motion caused by the natural flow of the club head as maximum speed is attained."

Ben Hogan: "To start the downswing, forget about the ... arms and hands."

Continued...

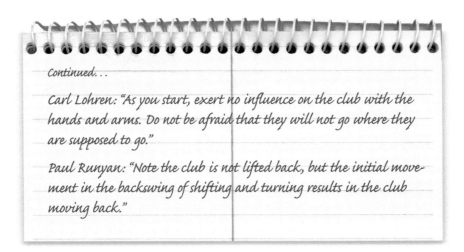

Continued...

Carl Lohren: "As you start, exert no influence on the club with the hands and arms. Do not be afraid that they will not go where they are supposed to go."

Paul Runyan: "Note the club is not lifted back, but the initial movement in the backswing of shifting and turning results in the club moving back."

In the past, Jack's arms (his *outside*) were moving on their own early in his backswing, and this would stop the coil that helps create power in the swing.

Old

New

Jack Nicklaus

You see, the less you turn your upper body going back, the less tension or coil you can create to use in the form of centrifugal force in the downswing. The smaller the upper body or coil going back, the slower the club head moves on the way forward. This is due to the loss of rotational force and angular momentum that can be created in the downswing when the backswing turn is completed. When golfers use their arms to make their backswing, they often do not complete the turn going back. This happens because the arms have gone up or back on their own, causing a false sense of a full backswing. This lack of a completed backswing results in a lack of coil that creates rotational forces and angular momentum.

The week before Jack Nicklaus won the 1986 Masters, the April 6 headline in the Augusta Chronicle *said, "Nicklaus takes game to lesson tee." The story told its readers that Nicklaus was on the practice range making a few swing correlations that he hoped would improve what he called "horrendous play this year." "Basically I've taken the hands out of my game," said Nicklaus. "I was playing with too much hands. I still want to win and think I can [and he did!]. I was lifting out of my plane on just about every backswing I made."*

Tom Watson told us, "I became a consistent driver only this year [1982]. In the past I would make a false turn because my hands started first, shoulders not turning enough—now I start everything that is away from the ball together. Arms close to body—now my swing is more efficient, arms and body in harmony." Tom also said, "On the course I'm reminding myself to have my arms closer to my body." The following thoughts from Tom Watson and Jack Nicklaus were found in *Golf Digest* articles from the 1980s.

The following excerpt is from *Medicine and Sports, Vol. 2*:

> With electronic testing of the muscles and high-speed motion picture analysis, it was found that average players, when compared to top-ranked players, fail to use momentum of the trunk and end up relying mostly on the arms, resulting also in not having as late or as rapid a release.

In 1946, Percy Boomer wrote, "From the shoulders, our power travels down through the arms, and as to arm action, I also believe the following common conception to be erroneous. Most people think they lift their arms to get them to the top of the backswing. With a modern [1946] controlled swing they do not lift—the arms work absolutely subjectively to the shoulders. That is why they are controlled. The triangle formed by our arms and the line between the shoulders should never lose its shape. It should be possible to push a wooden snooker triangle in between the arms and leave it there without impeding the swing, back or through. The arms have not been lifted; they have gone up in response to the shoulder movement. These are the basic movements of a connected and therefore controlled swing, and they must all be built into the framework of your feel of the swing."

Here is the triangle at address referred to by Percy Boomer. On page 24 you can see this triangle during the full swing.

The Triangle during the full swing.

Boomer continued, "If you keep these three basic feels, the pivot, the shoulders moving in response to the pivot and the arms moving in response to the shoulders, nothing much will go wrong with your game. So, we never have to consciously produce a good shot. We have to merely make certain movements which we have been taught and which will result in a good shot." He was talking about trusting your golf swing, and you can trust it if the *inside is moving the outside*.

Byron Nelson, discussing the discoveries that helped his game, made some comments that are both interesting and helpful. He talked about seeing pictures of leading amateur and professional golfers of his day "rolling their wrists" as the swing nears the ball. But as a result of a series of experiments, he found that when he did not try to roll his wrists and just let them stay in place for about 30 inches before impact and through the early stages of the follow through, he increased his accuracy.

Byron also talked about the best way to ensure a well-timed golf swing. He felt that one should start the backswing in a single motion with shoulders, hands, and club head moving together. Byron stopped trying to add extra movements to his hands (*outside*).

You have just read some thoughts from leaders in the world of golf on how the hands and arms should not be separated from your body. When they are, this may stop your game from reaching the level it is capable of reaching.

Remember, we would like your swing to be founded on the principles of rotational force and to have your *outside* (hands, arms, and club) moved by a transfer of weight created by your *inside* (your body). Angular momentum, inertia, centrifugal force, and kinetic energy can help you create a sound swing automatically.

See the Swing as a Wheel

It may be helpful to visualize the swing as a wheel with spokes. This can give you a little more understanding of how golf swing works and where power and energy come from when the swing is in motion. Picture the club head as the outermost part of a wheel (the rim). Next, picture the shaft of the club and your hands and arms as the spokes of this wheel. The hub, or center of the wheel, is your spine.

Science tells us that the most efficient way to start a wheel in motion—and have it stay on its axis—would be to apply force to its center or hub. This force then travels outward or is transmitted through the spokes to the outermost part of the wheel automatically.

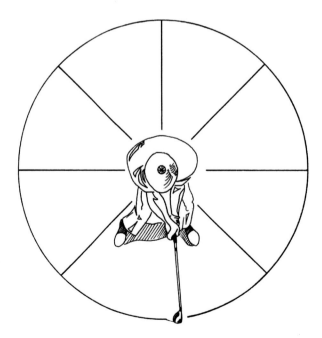

One of our goals in golf should be to make the most efficient swing possible and subconsciously repeat this swing as often as we can. A swing can be repeated if the hub of the swing is constant when the swing is in motion. In other words, I want the hub of the swing to revolve on its axis throughout the back-and-forth motion of the swing.

To keep the golf swing on its axis when it is in motion and keep the hub of the swing from changing position, start your "hub" or center of the swing moving first. This is the same motion as starting a wheel from its hub.

If you were to start your swing from your hands, or forearms, the swing would not start by first causing its hub to revolve. Instead, the joint just above the part that *is* used bends, and the subsequent movements leave the golf swing without extension or width:

- Moving the hands first could cause a wrist break or roll.
- Using the forearms could cause a bend at the elbow very early in the backswing.

Your goal is to have a swing that can repeat, and it *will* repeat when it stays on its axis. When the first move in the swing comes from its center, it can stay on its axis. The laws of physics and motion will help create a sound swing with power without any conscious use of your hands and arms when the *inside moves the outside*.

See It Work in Other Sports

Let's examine how the *inside moves the outside* in other popular and easy-to-recognize athletic movements. Your personal visualization should improve after reading this section!

Picture a major-league third baseman having a ground ball hit to him. He picks it up and makes a good throw to first base and the batter is out.

Now let's take a closer look at what he did with his body. As he bends down to field the ball, his chest, hips, and shoulders are all facing the ball (*opposite*, A pictures).

As the ball is picked up, his arms do not move, but his shoulders, chest, hips, and legs (*inside*) turn away from first base, and his arm (*outside*) and ball are moved behind him. The *inside* has moved the *outside* (B pictures).

Can you imagine the infielder making a throw by just moving his arm without turning his body? Not only would it look jerky, but also the throw would have no power. This occurs because when the arm (*outside*) moves on its own, there is no rotational force built up.

As the first baseman awaits the ball, he first sees the infielder's (*inside*) chest and finally the arm (*outside*) move under the influence of rotational force (C pictures).

Note how much faster his arm (*outside*) is moving than his body (*inside*). While the body made a somewhat smallish turn, look how far the hand (*outside*) traveled. The arms and chest stayed almost in the same position relative to one another during most of the throwing motion. You do not get the impression that the arm (*outside*) took off on its own at any time. In relation to the chest, it held almost the same position as when the ball was first picked up. Remember, if an athletic movement is under the influence of rotational force, the *outside* will be moved very fast even though the *inside* is moving more slowly.

When watching a big league pitcher, you also can see the body (*inside*) moving much slower than the arm (*outside*). Note how much the body (*inside*) is turned to the left of home plate after the pitch is delivered. In the attempt to move the ball forward, if at any point the body (*inside*) were to stop and the arm (*outside*) were to try and finish the action, the body (*inside*) would not be in a finished position that is easily recognized as such. The body must keep turning if the

arm is to have any speed or power, and it must also turn to the position where the right side is closer to home plate than the left side.

A right-handed golfer's sound, finished golf swing will have the right side closer to the target than the left. Ben Hogan told us how he wanted the swing to finish with the right side closer to the target. "At the completion of the swing, the player's belt buckle should definitely point to the left of his target (not directly at the target)."

In football, when the quarterback is about to receive the ball, his shoulders, chest, legs, and feet all are facing downfield. As he takes the football and steps back, the hands, arms, and ball are in the same position they were in when he first took the ball. Then the body (*inside*) starts to turn the arms and football back. The chest and shoulders turn away from downfield, carrying the arm and football back (*outside*). Then when the player wants the ball to go forward, the chest, shoulders, and finally the last part of the body—the arm (*outside*)—and ball are brought forward into the throwing position.

A tennis coach wants the tennis racket brought back by having the tennis player turning the (*inside*) chest and shoulders when making a ground stroke. If you were to stand directly in front of a tennis player who is serving, you would see the body (*inside*) turn forward, and in the trailing position, the arm and racket come forward. Imagine how awkward a serve would be if the arm and racket went forward without the body moving first!

When a baseball batter's swing starts forward, we can see the body (*inside*) start to turn. Then come the chest, the shoulders, and last, as in all other athletic motions under the influence of rotational force, the arms, hands, and bat.

This is also how a sound golf swing works. The less you use your hands and arms consciously, the more progress you will make with obtaining a sound golf swing. The arms and hands are being moved. They are moved under the influence of rotational force, which creates a load factor that in turn bends your wrists going back and again in the downswing with the stored-up power being released.

The Golf Swing in Motion

Before a swing can be considered sound, it must have what I call prerequisites. (Some of the following observations pertain to a right-handed golfer.)

1. The upper body starts the swing back.
2. The swing should have width and extension, with the club head traveling in the widest arc.
3. The club should move on a path or plane that is constant and can be repeated.
4. The backswing should create torque, windup, or coil.
5. The swing must transfer weight in a circle. Energy and power in sports is a transfer of weight with rotational forces. (You cannot transfer much weight with the *outside* arms and hands.)
6. The angle that is caused when the left wrist cocks during the backswing is held during the downswing by rotational forces.
7. The swing should finish with the right side closer to the target than the left, and the body should feel spent.
8. The golfer should have the feeling that he or she stays at the same height throughout the swing.
9. The arms should feel light and relaxed in the swing.
10. A golfer should feel that the club is the last thing to move or that it has been left behind as the swing moves down plane toward the ball.

The golf swing's assignment is to swing the club on a path that has a relationship to a target.

The golfer's responsibility is to develop a simple system that can meet this assignment.

Getting the swing in motion (or the backswing), in my view, starts from above the waist, without the use of the hands and arms. When you are standing to the ball correctly (we will cover this later), all I want you to do is to turn your shoulder and upper body back. Because all golfers will not feel the swing in the same way, your concept of how to do this may be different from your neighbor's. If we were to take pictures of several golfers, all making a good or sound backswing, there would be a good chance all would have a different key to making the back move. *The important point is not to do anything with your hands or arms!*

You may want to start your swing by turning your back to the target or by having the feeling of turning your chest over your right foot. Someone else may turn their right shoulder around their neck. (Arnold Palmer used this thought at one time.) Some golfers picture a triangle made up of the shoulders and two arms, and they just turn this triangle back with the upper body. The suggestion Carl Lohren uses is to start the swing with the left shoulder area. Because we play golf with our nervous system, it is my opinion that there has to be some personal discovery before you find the best visualization for the start of your personal backswing. Just make sure there is a weight transfer, and do not use your arms or hands or have the feeling you are going either up or down with your body.

The Backswing Is Only Inches Long

When you start your swing without the arms and the upper body (*inside*) has done its job, and you are in the full coil position with your back facing the target—you have only moved a few inches, not even a foot! Look at the spot where the left shoulder started in the swing and the spot where it stops at the end of the coil. It has only moved inches. The backswing is only a few inches long, and no longer. In his research, D. S. Meyer showed that in the full golf swing, the club head covers about 27 feet. He is talking about the club head moving 27 feet; remember the club head is part of the "*outside*." Remember our example using the yardstick? When you move your upper body (*inside*) inches on the backswing, the club head travels many times that amount. Picture your chest as a mirror; the club head would be reflected in that mirror for most of the backswing. While the club head (*outside*) has traveled a great distance, the *inside* has only moved a few inches.

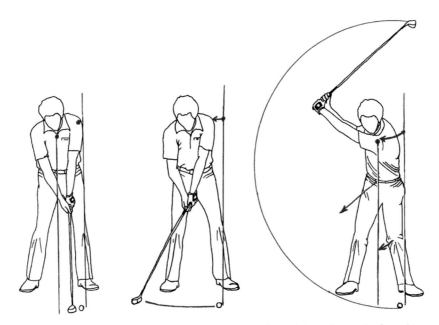

While the club head outside has traveled a great distance, the inside has only moved a few inches.

If your visualizations and concepts about the backswing have been larger or bigger than inches, you are making your backswing more complicated than it has to be. Picture the backswing as small or short, and the club will go to the finish of your backswing. The end of the backswing should be visualized as a spot that most golfers think of as the halfway point of the backswing. The reason the club goes to the position we normally picture or call the finish of the backswing is because of momentum and the load factor, not because we swing it there. When the *inside is turning the outside*, the club head is being moved under the influence of rotational force and is picking up speed and momentum.

When the club head reaches what we would normally call halfway back, with our coil or turn completed, the club head (*outside*) keeps going back because of momentum, and the load factor causes the club to cock the wrists. The arms have done nothing. The hands have done nothing. For most of the backswing the arms have moved because the *inside* moved them, but in the final stage of the backswing, the arms and hands are moving into the top backswing position because of momentum and load factor. Don't try to control this move! Influence the size of your coil and not what the arms and hands are doing. Let them do their thing! Let them feel free of control.

Example: When looking at that ice-skating line going around and around, if the inside person were to suddenly stop, do you think the outside person would stop at the same time? No! The outside person would keep moving for a short time. This is because of momentum and load factor. The same action occurs in a sound golf swing. Most golfers have a backswing that is too long. You should now have some understanding of why this happens. When you try to swing the club all the way back to the spot you previously accepted as the top or end of the backswing, the club travels beyond that point due to the laws of physics and momentum. The overswing is caused by poor visualization of the backswing compounded by the hands and arms swinging the club back rather than the *inside* bringing the club back. Remember, the backswing is only a few inches long!

Here is an illustration of what happens in a sound swing. When you try to swing to position A, the club, hands, and arms will travel to position B automatically when the inside is moving the outside.

In my case, consciously manipulating the hands and wrists at any point in the backswing is a sure way to shift the club head out of its proper path.
—Past U.S. Open Champion

I imagined my upper arms were literally strapped tight to the sides of my chest.
—Past Masters Champion

During the swing, the club is either on plane or it is off plane. In a sound swing the club is on plane.
—Hank Haney

The backswing can lose its width and extension if you try to do something with your hands or arms when taking the club back. When the upper body (*inside*) creates the backswing, the club will stay on its proper path or plane. This is the line or path the club must travel on if we are to have a swing that will repeat and can be trusted. In a sound swing, the arms stay on the chest. Trust just letting the arms move with your upper body's turn. Have the feeling that your upper arms are staying on your chest during the backswing. Think of it as though your upper arms were surgically sewn to your chest! If they do leave this position, it is only slightly and only for a moment. But preferably, you should feel both arms close to the chest in the backswing with the left arm never moving off the chest at any time during the backswing.

Swing Path or Plane

A sound golf swing will stay on its plane when in motion. At address, your arms are extended at an angle. The degree of this angle depends on the size and posture of the golfer. A tall golfer will have a more perpendicular or upright angle. Our shorter golfer will have a flatter or more acute angle. Your posture and the golf club define the plane or path your swing should follow. If you were to see a golfer making a shot where the ball was waist high (off a side hill lie or stuck in a bush or tree), you would see a swing that would go back and forth or around the spine—the golfer's spine is perpendicular to the ground during this type of shot.

When the golfer hits a ball on the ground, his spine tilts over, giving the impression that the club is going up. Actually, the club is traveling on the same angle/path to the spine as when the golfer was standing straight up for the waist-high shot—back and forth or around. The person who feels that the club has gone up is being misled by what he sees, because the club *should* be traveling on a path around the spine, and the degree of tilt in the spine causes the shape of the swing that our eyes see. Swings with longer clubs will look more "around" than swings with shorter clubs. The more we tilt or bend over, the more "up" the swing will look. Do not be misled; *the sound swing is always on its plane moving in an arc around the spine*.

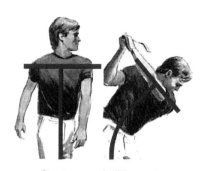

Picturing your shoulders turning around your spine can be helpful.

Clubs are designed with a shaft that site on a roof-like inclined plane when they are correctly placed behind the ball at address.

If the swing keeps the club shaft parallel to the original shaft angle seen at address, it is on plane.

When the swing is on plane, the arms stay in front of the body, arms and elbows somewhat together.

The Plane

Notice:
The angle of the shaft, when it is soled correctly at address, is similar to the angle of a roof of a house.

Suggestion:
Sound swings keep the club shaft on plane throughout the swing.

Visualize:
The shaft is either pointing to or parallel to the bottom of the plane during a sound swing.

I stand tall, then stay tall. I maintain my weight in the hips, shoulders,and head throughout the swing.
—Past T.P.C. Champion

Short

(A)

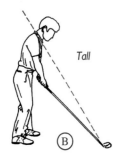

Tall

(B)

(C)

We ask golfers to picture the "Hogan Visualization" of the glass plate that sits across his shoulders at the angle that is caused by his posture. This plate of glass defines the path of Hogan's shoulder plane. When he made his swing, his shoulders traveled just under the glass, as yours will do if you do nothing with your hands and arms.

By just turning your upper body, the club travels on its plane automatically. It can go on this path when it is under the influence of rotational force and momentum. The main cause of a club moving off its plane is the arms making an extra move in the backswing. *When starting the backswing, do not go up or down with your body or arms.*

When the *outside* (hands and arms) does nothing but lets itself be turned by the *inside* (upper body), the club will stay on its swing plane because matter, once moving, if kept moving, will stay on its path, unless affected by an outside force.

When a golfer sets up correctly—bending from the hips, tilting the spine, flexing the knees, head off the chest—and stays in this posture throughout the swing, it will help keep the club on plane or in its correct path.

When the club is on plane at the top of the backswing:

- your left wrist is flat and in line with the back of the left hand;
- the face of the club is square, and the left arm is parallel to the angle the shaft occupied at address; and
- the shaft is parallel to both the ground and the target line.

Plane Visualization

When the swing is on plane the right palm faces up and the left palm faces down.

Off Plane   **On Plane**

Off Plane   **On Plane**

On Plane

When the shaft of the club is parallel to the target line as the swing gets waist high in both the down and backswing, **the club is on plane**.

When the grip end of the club points at the target line when the swing is between waist high and the top of the swing, **the club is on plane**.

When a golfer lets his hands, arms, and club respond to "the inside" or "hub," there is an in-plane roll of the left arm caused by the design of the club.

Research tells us: It seems certain that the key in getting to the correct top-of-back-swing position is the first foot or so of the backswing. If this is correct, the rest of the backswing will tend to follow naturally. This is why some professionals so often advise a "one-piece take-away."

The design of the golf club and the versatile joint of the left shoulder tend to roll the arm. This 30° roll of the left arm is natural or automatic unless the golfer interferes.

The movements happen quite naturally if they are given the chance to. The simple in-plane roll and cocking of the wrist is merely the natural conclusion, caused by the backswing momentum of the club and the way the left shoulder joint works.

The club head also follows the whole hub action during the early stages of the downswing. It is the hub action that sets the plane pattern and timing of the swing down, not the hands and arms. During the downswing the wrist is not only uncocking, but is also rotating along with the left forearm back on its own axis. As with the backswing, the roll happens *automatically* because of the in-plane momentum of the club head. When power comes from *unforced* wrist action (whether uncocking or rolling), it is merely helping the natural out-swinging action (of the club head) that had its origin at the hub of the swing.

A full coil of the upper body will be created when the upper body (*inside*) is given the responsibility of creating the backswing. There are two common ways of preventing coil. The first cause is the over use of the lower body in the back-swing. The lower body should move a shorter distance than the upper body.

Overuse of the lower body can cause the center of gravity to move past our base of support. Upper body has moved more than the lower and the right leg has stayed in place.

It should feel as though you are moving your upper body against the lower body, similar to winding up a child's toy. If the toy were to move in the same direction or distance as the key you are turning, the toy's spring would not wind up.

I like to tell golfers to feel like they keep the lower body out of the backswing. The turn of the upper body will naturally pull the lower body into the action of the backswing just enough. When throwing a ball a short distance, our legs and hips are moved a very short distance. When the throw is going to be longer, the legs and hips are moved a larger distance. This happens because of the bigger upper body coil caused by wanting to throw the ball a longer distance.

Muscles of the lower back are attached to the hip area of the body and pull the lower body into the backswing. In sports it is very natural to let the lower body follow the upper body going backward, so let's use the same system for your golf swing. Your lower body will naturally move the correct amount during the coil back, you don't think very much about it.

A visualization that has helped many golfers is to have the feeling that the right leg does not move in the backswing. It may move a small amount, but the movement will stay to a minimum by trying not to move the leg at all.

Also, as a result of a proper coil, the left knee will point back to the ball (see illustrations *opposite*). Another good visualization is that golf is played inside the feet. In the backswing, your body or the weight that is going backwards should not go outside your right foot.

The same is true for the downswing, during this part of the swing, your body weight should not pass your left foot. Play golf inside your feet. When the right leg in place, the swing will stay inside the right foot nicely.

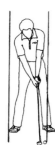

The head may also turn slightly during the backswing. If the head does not turn, it makes it almost impossible to have any weight move back on the right side. The movement is very small, but it should be part of the backswing. I also like to have golfers keep their weight a little more to the heels during the backswing.

✓ **Try this exercise and you will see why. Put your body in the position where you are about to throw a ball forward. Your upper body is turned away from your target, with your arm back. At this point your weight will be on your right heel. Hold that position and move the weight off your right heel to your right toe. You will start to lose your balance. Now put the weight back on your heel. You are now back in a balanced and powerful position to move forward.**

The second way of destroying a good coil is to have your arms (*outside*) move on their own anywhere in the backswing. This is what Jack Nicklaus and Tom Watson found happening to their swings a few years ago. Their coil was not what they were looking for. With the arms taking over the backswing, their arms would try to finish the backswing. Both told us that the body would

stop turning because of a false sense of having made a completed backswing when the arms got to the top on their own. Your backswing will have coil, width, extension, and stay in its plane when you do nothing with your arms (*outside*) and just let them be moved back by the upper body (*inside*). Also, please remember to picture the backswing as inches in size, not several feet.

Note how the right leg does not move very much in a sound backswing and that the left knee is pointing back past the ball.

Full Swing Visualization

The drawings of the full swing on the opposite page are what most golfers would use as a model of the positions a sound golf swing goes through. All the easy-to-recognize positions (hands, arms, and club) can be seen.

It is my opinion that golfers will only confuse themselves, or make progress with their swing harder than it has to be, if they are concerned with what the hands and arms are doing in the swing.

These drawings (*opposite*) are of Ben Hogan, but a picture of any sound swing can give the impression the golf swing is large. But the swing is very small when the *inside is moving the outside*.

There is no need to picture an exact swing in your mind. You should only be concerned with swinging the club and what the body does to accomplish the movement of weight—not what the hands and arms are doing.

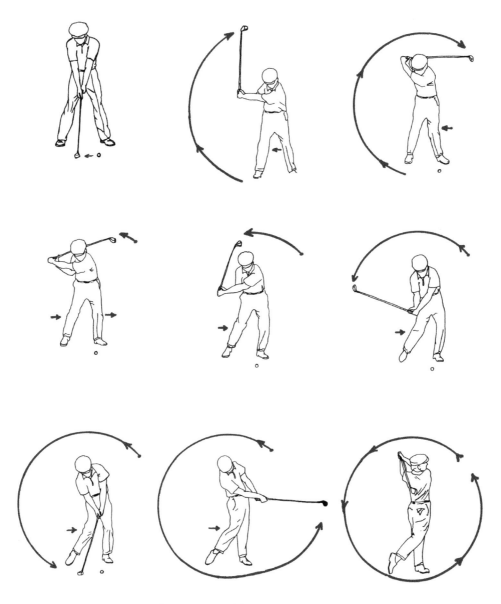

Forget the arms and let the inside move the outside!

Visualizing the Swing Without the Hands, Arms, and Club

The illustration below shows Ben Hogan's swing (also seen on *previous page*) without the hands, arms, and club. You can see how small the golf swing really is when the hands, arms, and club are not part of your visualization.

For some golfers it may be more helpful to be able to recognize what the body or *inside* does during the swing than to have a picture of the hands and arms in your mind. Please don't try and do anything extra with them during the swing.

Recognize how small the golf swing is. The hands, arms and club (*outside*) are moved as a unit a great distance by the body (*inside*) that has rotated only inches while creating rotational force.

Even in Sand, the
Inside Moves the Outside

When you see pictures of a good sand player you can see the hands and arms being moved as a unit by the *inside*.

The unit of the hands and arms can be pictured as a triangle that does not travel on its own during the swing. Notice how the upper arms stay on the chest throughout the swing as the *inside moves the outside*.

When the sand shot requires a lot of height, there is sometimes a small wrist break at the start, but the wrist break does not always start the sand shot.

Leave the Club Behind

The inside moves the outside, and it can be seen in all sports—golf is not the exception. If you have been playing golf for a while, it may not be easy for you to accept such a simple thought! You may have worked very hard to make progress using other tips and suggestions and find it's hard to accept that you do not have to think about your arms.

Of all the statements that are being shared with you, there is one that may give you the most understanding to what happens in the sound golf swing. Bobby Jones said, "The all important feel which I experience as the swing changes direction is that I have the distinct feeling that I have left the club behind as I start forward." May I repeat that: "The all important feel which I experience as the swing changes direction is that I have the distinct feeling that I have left the club behind as I start forward."

Look at any athlete in motion, and you can see the arm, hands, and whatever else is being held has been left behind as the motion starts forward.

The baseball pitcher, the batter, the quarterback, the tennis player, the infielder, all look as though the arm has been left behind as the body starts forward. As the *inside* turns, the *outside* is finally brought to its full speed and power after being left behind.

When looking at the sound golf swing, it too looks like the arm and club have been left behind. It looks this way because that is what is happening. In the sound swing, the arms do not move on their own. They are pulled by the force that has been built up by the *inside* rotating them down to impact.

Use this as a swing key. Try to leave your arms behind when you start your downswing. They will come down at the correct time, not before, when you try your best to keep them out of the swing.

If the arms were to push, this would be like the outside skater on the skate line letting go of the line and trying to skate alone. If the rotational force in the golf swing were interrupted, the energy of this natural power would be lost, and motion could only continue artificially, with the hands (*outside*) trying to hit.

Watching the arms in the swing of a good player, I feel, is not as helpful to your visualization as looking at the movements of the club. Over the years, I have found that when golfers try to leave the club behind, several important and required results in the swing are taken care of automatically.

One important result of leaving the club behind is that the right shoulder is lowered and the plane of the swing is constant. The club is now approaching the ball from inside the target line and will produce a squaring clubface through impact. This happens without any use of the hands because the golfer has let the shoulder rotation lead the downswing and has left the hands and club behind.

Also, the inside path of the club head assures that the body's leverage and force will be behind the hit, giving your swing the ability to generate maximum force. (To move an object forward, you must be behind it.)

The change of direction from back to down happens slowly in a sound golf swing. A good swing key is to change direction slowly and do not try to roll your hands through impact. They are moved as a unit by the inside. Sometimes it looks like they roll, but that is because of the angle you are looking from. I will expand upon that statement later in the book.

Below, each A picture is the top or finish of the backswing. In the B photos, you can clearly see the body has rotated forward while the (*outside*) hands, arms, and club have been left behind.

A golfer's downswing must also stay on its plane or path, have width or extension (in fact, have expanding extension), and finish on balance with the right side closer to the target than the left. I have found that all of these prerequisites will occur when the arms do nothing consciously in the downswing.

☑   **The downswing can feel the same speed as the backswing. Do not try to make the downswing go faster; don't try and add speed. When you let the body or weight transfer (*inside*), bring the hands, arms, and club down, they will have unbelievable power and speed because they are being moved under the Laws of Motion. The change of direction (when the swing stops going back and starts down) is slow in a sound swing.**

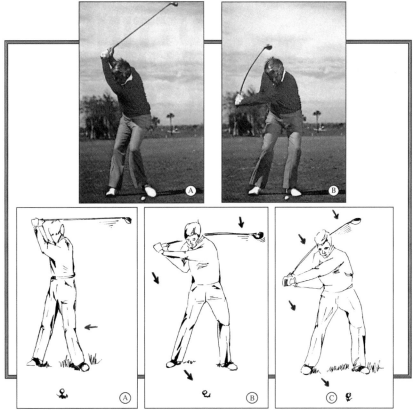

Downward pressure causes the shaft to flex down in the downswing when the inside is moving the outside. This pressure is then applied to the ball.

Earlier in this book, I explained *angular momentum*: It is the rotation of matter or mass around its axis or center. One of the golf swing's "axis" of rotation is our spine, or a line midway between the shoulders. The "mass" of the swing is made up of the body, shoulders, arms, hands, and club. At the top of the backswing part of the mass (the club) moves in close to the axis of the swing, our spine. The right arm is flexed and is close, and the left arm could not be closer. Then force is created when the shoulder turn (rotational action) starts the swing going down to impact.

As the club is being swung downward, its weight begins to expand the wrist cock and right arm away from the axis of the body. This is a result of the rotational forces that are being created by the *inside moving the outside* and

The outside...

thus causing an expansion of the angles created in the backswing. As the downswing continues, the hands, arms, and club keep moving further from the axis and a transfer of momentum starts to first slow down your arms, then your hands just as predicted by a law of physics. The momentum of the arms and hands moves out into the club head and creates power and club head speed automatically without any conscious effort by the golfer. Keep in mind, the tip end of a whip gets its speed from the handle rotating.

...is expanding. A very good swing thought is to feel the arms are very light during the swing.

When a golf swing has a transfer of momentum, the hands are actually slowing down when the ball is hit. Some golfers feel the hands are, or should be, speeding up at this point; they are not—in a sound golf swing the hands are no longer accelerating. Like the tip end of a whip, the club head now has all the momentum, speed, and energy.

The Target Turn

Your right shoulder moves your right elbow down plane. This moves the lower spine forward to the back of the ball before the hip turn starts.

In my opinion, the body will always turn—it is a natural tendency. Some golfers will turn too soon, some too late. Others do not turn enough, but there always is some semblance of a turn in the downswing. Because there is some type of turn going on, a good key to have is to just go down plane with your right shoulder, and after you start going down, the natural tendency to turn will become part of the downswing. In all sound swings, the lower spine moves forward as the body starts to turn (see A, B, and C, *below*). Just let the right shoulder go down plane and the rest will take care of itself. Keep the *inside* moving until the right side is closer to the target than the left.

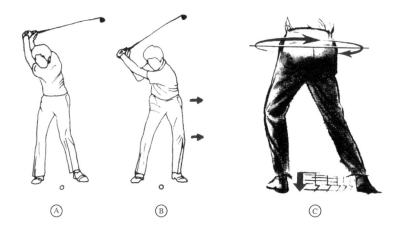

Lag—Drag—Pressure—No Slack

Lag, *drag*, *pressure*, and *no slack* are other conditions that exist in all sound golf swings when a golfer leaves the club behind (avoiding any conscious use of the hands and arms). For no slack to be present in a swing, the body rotation would have to start forward before the club starts back down to impact. This move starts the downswing in a tight sequence, preventing any slack from entering the swing. When the body starts its rotation forward, this causes two other needed conditions to occur. First, this body rotation helps add to the wrist flex that happens in the backswing. It also puts downward pressure on the club's shaft that can now be transferred as pressure on the ball as it is hit. A sound swing always puts pressure on the ball, compressing it onto the clubface. This pressure comes from the downward pressure that started to load up the shaft in the first stage of the downswing and body rotation.

This same kind of pressure can be seen building up in a fly rod shaft as the handle of the rod changes directions to move the hook and line forward into the water. When the left wrist is fully flexed and the club's shaft has the needed pressure on it, now all the sound golf swing has to do is drag the club head down to the ball. The sound golf swing leaves the club behind and the laws of motion help bring it down to impact, giving the feeling of lagging and dragging the club through impact.

On page 55, positions A show the top or finish of the backswing. In the B positions, you can clearly see the body has rotated, while the (*outside*) hands, arms, and club have been left behind.

Retain the Angle

In Ben Hogan's swing and in any efficient golf swing, there are two positions I would like to point out. One is of the master at the top of his swing, and the other is his swing as it moves into the impact area of the swing. In A (*below*), the hands and arms are back. In B, they are about to unload all the power of the swing through the ball. The hands, arms, and club have moved a good distance, but as Hogan tells us, he has done nothing with the arms or club. In fact, he said to forget the arms when making your swing. He has moved his *inside* (body rotation)! This is a pure example of the *inside moving the outside*. The club has traveled several feet, while the right shoulder has moved only a short distance.

Retain the angle, some books and golf instructors correctly suggest. During the downswing, they want golfers not to change the angle or position that the hands and wrists fall into at the top of the backswing until the impact area. In my view,

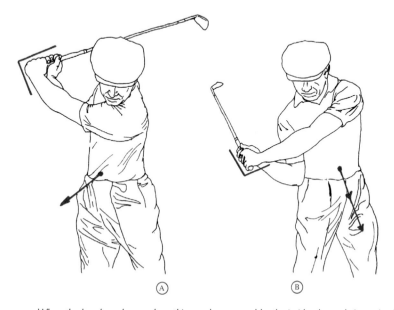

When the hands and arms do nothing and are moved by the inside, the angle is retained.

when you do nothing consciously with the hands, arms, and club in the downswing, this important move of retaining the angle is automatically accomplished. The only time the angle breaks down is when the golfer tries to do something with the swing besides rotating with the *inside* or body. This alignment that the hands, arms, and club fall into at the top does not change until the rotational force that is influencing the downswing causes the club to expand the left wrist and right arms and whack the hell out of the ball. The rotational force that we are talking about is created by the *inside body moving the outside body*.

You can clearly see the hands, arms and club stay in the same position in both the A and B sketches. It is almost as though a the sketch were a toy that had been be moved into different positions by putting one's fingers on the golfer's shoulder and turning the shoulders back to the point they were in for picture A. The hands, arms, and club have been swung as a unit by the *inside*. They have not moved on their own. Please also note that the hands are almost the same distance from the shoulder in both pictures, and that the angle of the wrists has not changed in either picture.

The position the club, hands, and arms fall into at the top of the swing does not change in a sound golf swing until rotational forces expand them. Because of rotational force at the point of ball contact in a good swing, the arms are being expanded, fully stretched out, coming to a relaxed and spent position behind the body at the end of the swing.

At impact with the golf ball, the club head has most of the energy of the swing, This happens because the power created by rotational force has moved outward and into the club head from the body. Because of this, you should have the feeling that the club head is now pulling you around to the finished balanced position, with the body feeling relaxed and spent with most of your weight on the front foot. Do not force the finish; let it happen as a result of doing nothing consciously with the *outside*. The rotational force, created by the *inside*, will cause the finish of your swing.

Some golf instruction over the years has suggested that golfers should swing their arms freely through the ball, that the arms should start the downswing. From my point of view, the arms are moved freely, and there is a big difference between moving your arms and having them moved freely.

Please look at these sketches of a good swing, and observe that the space between the right shoulder and the hands looks like it gets larger as the swing moves down to impact from A to B. Some instruction says that this is proof that the arms start the swing forward. Yes, the space does appear to increase, but you can be misled by what you think you are seeing. From the front angle, or looking from the position facing the golfer's chest and waist, it does appear that the space gets much larger, but it is an optical illusion!

Note how the unit (hands, arms, and club) stays in place as transferring weight or rotation moves it downward. This unit does not move on its own.

When the downswing is well on its way (B) the right arm is still folded at the same angle as it was at the top of the swing. Also, the hands are almost the same distance from the right shoulder as they were at the top. What has happened is that the hands, arms, and club, as a unit, have been swung downward by a transfer of weight that comes from rotating the right shoulder down plane.

When describing his downswing at the halfway point, Ben Hogan said, "My arms are in the same relative position as they were at the top of the swing. My body did its work on the downswing by pulling the arms and hands into position. Forget about your arms, hands, and club when starting the downswing."

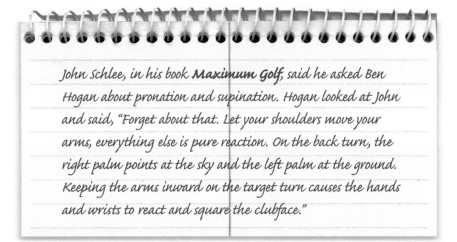

John Schlee, in his book **Maximum Golf***, said he asked Ben Hogan about pronation and supination. Hogan looked at John and said, "Forget about that. Let your shoulders move your arms, everything else is pure reaction. On the back turn, the right palm points at the sky and the left palm at the ground. Keeping the arms inward on the target turn causes the hands and wrists to react and square the clubface."*

Do not be misled. It is just the angle you are watching from. Look at the swing from in back of or behind the golfer, and you can see the hands stay in the same relative position to the right shoulder until the expanding action from rotational forces take over. As the swing moves down toward ball contact (C), the arms begin to expand or stretch out to an expanded position. Keep in mind that rotational forces are an expanding force, and the arms of a golfer expand for the same reason a baseball pitcher's arm expands. The body (*inside*) is doing its job of rotation and transferring force that causes the natural results of the laws of physics to take place. Also (C) the hands, arms, and club start to swing down very powerfully, again a natural result of the *inside moving the outside*, not because the golfer is trying to swing his arms fast. Angular momentum is doing its part at this point in the swing, and this is another reason there is no need to try and do anything with your hands or arms during the swing.

No Rollover!

From my point of view, the progress you are capable of in golf will not take place until there are visualizations of the golf swing in your mind's eye that are helpful—visualizations that will not mislead!

The subject of wrist flex and elbow fold that takes place as the swing moves backwards has been widely discussed. For the most part, the teaching and coaching community universally accept this action and why it happens. This flex or fold during the backswing is one part of the golf swing that has caused little or no controversy over the years. However, as the swing moves down, the movements or positions the hands, arms, and wrists go through have been the cause of discussion and debate for years.

Terms are sometimes held on to out of convenience, or a term has been in use for such a long time that more harm than good would come out of a changing the particular term. "The right hand rolls over the left" is a saying that has been in use for a long time. In this case, those are possible reasons that these descriptions are still widely used and believed. However—perhaps the strongest case for using these descriptions—it is said that these actions can be seen when looking at pictures of the swing. Golfers will also say they can feel *roll* happen.

With all the respect I have for all the men and women who teach and coach this game we all love and for the golfers who are working hard to improve, I would ask them all to take a closer look at pictures of the swing, and just maybe, the statements about rolling the hands would change.

I feel that golf is being made harder than it has to be when instruction suggests golfers should be rolling hands. Yes, there is movement in the hands during the swing, but it is not a rollover! In a sound golf swing, the movements that do occur are happening automatically. Golfers are not required to make or to put any conscious effort into making these natural movements occur. There is a natural in-plane rotation of the arms and club in a sound swing.

Address Position

Everyone agrees that the first change we can see is when the right elbow folds as the backswing is reaching its halfway point.

At the top of the swing the wrist and club can fall into one of three positions—square, open, or closed. The club head moving off center (or off plane) causes two of these positions: open or closed.

The club head is square when club head weight is on center or on its plane and club shaft is pointing forward or straight with little or no in or out bend in the wrist.

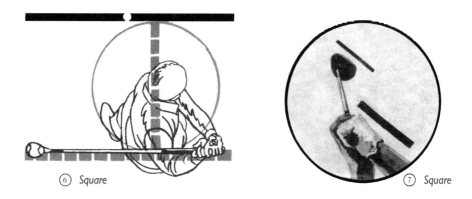

⑥ *Square*   ⑦ *Square*

The open position exists when club head weight is to the right of center. Club shaft points right and left wrist bends right.

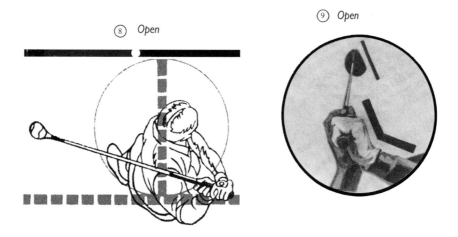

⑧ *Open*   ⑨ *Open*

The closed position exists when the club head weight is to the left of center. The club shaft points left, and the wrist bends left.

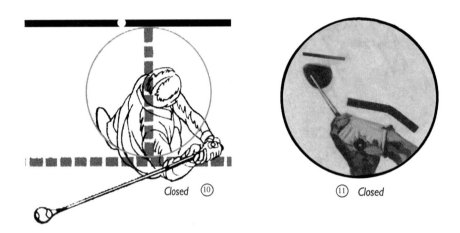

Closed ⑩   ⑪ *Closed*

The club head can move off center or off its plane for several reasons (which we will not go into at this time). But what would be helpful for you to recognize is that the wrists are flexible and respond to where the club is and to the laws of physics and motion. They will bend in the direction of the club weight and toward where the shaft is pointing because of their flexibility.

Bending the left wrist during the backswing also occurs during the downward motion. Wrists do not roll, but they will bend left or right of center when the laws of motion cause the flexible wrists to follow the lead of club head weight and shaft. It is left or right of center, not roll, that takes place when swing is in motion.

Now let's look at a sound swing as it moves down, and you can see the right hand is still on top because the weight of the club is still on center (or on plane).

As the swing moves to knee or thigh height, the right hand can still be seen on top of the left.

At impact, the right hand is still on top because the club is still on center.

Sam Snead told John Schlee that he played his best golf when his wrists felt "dead" and that the cocked wrists are along for the ride (see picture 1, *page 64*).

As the swing gets waist high, the right hand may look like it's starting to roll over the left. This is the position that is most often used to show the right is going "over" the left. The right—as we can see—is higher than the left, but do not be misled. Remember the position the right hand was in at the start of the swing (higher than left). It's still in that same higher position; it has not changed. But when looking at pictures of the swing we can be misled into thinking or seeing something that really did not happen—roll (see pictures 1 [*page 64*] and 18 [*below*]). Also, the club is rising at this point in the swing, which could give the impression the right hand is moving up and over.

During the next stages of the downswing, the rotational force created by the rotational movement of the swing starts to influence the club head for the same reasons it did during the backswing and the club head will start moving left of center. The slinging action of the swing—rotational force—is causing this movement to the left by the club head, bending the flexible wrist in the same direction. The wrists are not rolling. Again, from some angles, it may look like they are—and maybe feel like they are—but they are following the laws of motion and are bending left of center.

A closer look at the position the club, hands, and wrists are falling into will show the right hand's position in relation to the left (on top) has not changed. We can also see that the left wrist is bending in the direction of the club head weight. Left of center—*not* a roll.

The laws of motion that cause the golf club to move left of center after impact are the same laws that cause the tip end of a whip to move past the rest of the whip for a short time before the whip becomes fully extended. In an ice show, this same result can be seen when the outside person on a skate line is moved past the rest of the line (as the skater is whipped forward) for a short time just before the line becomes straight. The club head is like the tip end of a whip and is responding to the laws of motion when it moves off center—to the left—during the downswing.

About halfway through the follow-through, as the swing keeps rotating, the club head will move back on center, and we no longer will see any bend in the wrists. This happens because during this stage of the swing, the club head is slowing down, and the rotating body has again caught up with the club head causing the wrist to come back on center again.

If a golfer has a full finish, the club head responds to the rotation action of a full finish and causes the wrists to bend once again as the swing moves into its final stages.

If the hands did roll in the downswing (right over left), how would the hands finish in their familiar right under left position at the completion of the swing?

When the laws of motion are influencing the swing, your shots will be straight or may have a slight draw without trying to roll. For a short time, the arms of a golfer with a sound swing move closer together during the downswing. This is caused by the outward pull of the club head, expansion, angular momentum, and rotational forces.

You can see the arms move together—a result of the laws of motion—in pictures of a sound swing. But during the finish of a swing, the arms will move away or separate from each other once again because the outward pull of the club head, angular momentum, and rotational force are no longer influencing the swing as the golfer comes to a spent and relaxed finish.

There are times when a golfer will try to roll his or her hands or arms to give the ball a big hook. But when your swing is responding to the laws of motion with the inside moving the outside, the hands, wrists, and club—without any conscious effort—will fall into all the expected and accepted positions.

In closing, for you to be able to make progress with your golf game, you must first see the swing correctly in your mind's eye. If you have been seeing a roll, you may be making golf harder than it has to be.

Part II

Observations for Your Progress

Understanding your goals beforehand will help with any endeavor you may choose. Golf is no exception.

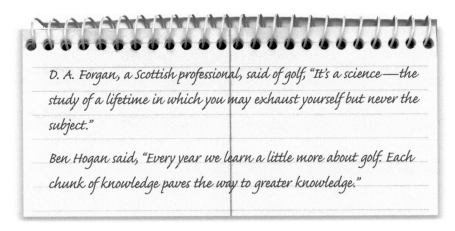

D. A. Forgan, a Scottish professional, said of golf, "It's a science — the study of a lifetime in which you may exhaust yourself but never the subject."

Ben Hogan said, "Every year we learn a little more about golf. Each chunk of knowledge paves the way to greater knowledge."

Base or Fixed Point

Your target turn needs a base of support or fixed point to move around. In a sound golf swing this base is the left foot. This is a base that can be seen in all sports. The left foot either anchors or gives the needed support for rotational movements in sports. Try to turn without first establishing a base of support for the turning and weight transfer that should be present (but this will be very hard to complete if the left foot is not in place first).

Some of golf's outstanding players keep their left foot in place during the backswing. You may want to try this, but if you find this does not fit your style, please be sure to return your left foot to the ground to support your forward turn.

In baseball, remember how slowly the body of the batter, pitcher, or fielder is rotating and how fast the hands and arms are being moved. This visualization can help your golf swing.

The Head

If your head moves back a little during the backswing, this is very acceptable. It is hard to make a backswing that transfers weight with the head perfectly steady. In fact, some golfers may find themselves making what they feel is a very acceptable backswing, but most of their weight will still be forward if their head does not move back a little. A very common fault among recreation golfers is trying to keep the head still during the backswing. Do not try to move the head—let nature take its course.

During the downswing, your head stays back as the body rotation swings the club down to impact. The head is a fulcrum of the swing.

Example 1: Picture a baseball player's head going forward with the bat as he makes his swing. If his head goes with his arms and bat as his body turns, the swing will have little power. With the head back, acting as the swing's fulcrum, the bat receives the energy of rotational force and has plenty of power.

Example 2: Picture a hammer in use with the handle and head both moving in the same direction as you try to hit something. There would be little power. The handle is the fulcrum; therefore, to create any energy, it must stay (lag) behind as the head passes it.

The same is true of the golf swing. A fulcrum—the golfer's head—stays back until the ball is on its way. It comes forward because of the pulling energy of rotational force. Your head comes forward only after the ball is on its way and feels like you are swinging past your head.

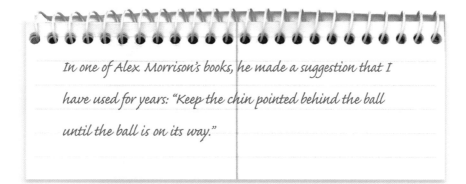

In one of Alex Morrison's books, he made a suggestion that I have used for years: "Keep the chin pointed behind the ball until the ball is on its way."

ROTATE: The right side is closer to the target than the left.

Looking at the Swing
from Behind Can Help

The opposite page is an illustration of Bobby Nichols's swing—but anyone's sound swing could have been used.

Note sketches 1 and 9: They are the same, but 1 is at address, while 9 is at ball contact.

Note pictures 3 and 8: They are the same, but 3 is on the way back, while 8 is in the downswing.

Note pictures 4 and 7: They are the same, but 4 is on the way back, while 7 is in the downswing.

Note pictures 1–10: The hand and arms (*the outside*) are in the same relative position as the upper body (*the inside*).

It might be helpful to picture the hands, arms, and club as one unit—let's say you envision the letter *Y*, or a triangle. You can see that the unit does not move on its own—the unit is moved by the *inside* and stays in place because of inertia.

Yes, the hands fall under the club at the top and the arms expand during the down-swing. But this happens and is caused by the laws of motion that influence a sound golf swing. Golfers do not have to do anything consciously with their hands and arms. They should just trust and let *the inside move the outside*. The unit of hands, arms, and club will be moved back and forth during the swing and keep the same relative position it was in at address by the transfer of weight created by the actions of the *inside*.

We can see the same position in the back and downswings, because the position the hands, arms, and club take at address stays in place and is just moved back and forth by the *inside* (torso).

Standing to the Ball, Balance, Counterbalance, and Low Center of Gravity

At address, your body should be somewhat relaxed. Any tension will negate the movement of weight your swing is trying to transfer back and forth.

I like to have golfers stand with their feet wide enough apart to support the weight shift, which is wider than most people think it is. It will only be too wide if your feet are outside your shoulders. Stand nice and wide, with knees pointed slightly to the target, left foot turned out, and right foot square. When the setup is complete, I like the weight to be more to the heels than the toes and slightly more to the left side (for a right-handed golfer) for irons and to the right side for woods. Your legs should maintain a flex at the knees for balance.

The buttocks extend past the heels only a few inches as the upper body bends over the hips with the back somewhat straight (it feels like squatting slightly).

The hands and arms move off the body as it bends over. Gravity causes them to hang straight down from the shoulders during the bend. The upper arms stay on the chest. Keep the chin up. The chin should not move closer to the chest when bending over at address. If it does, the chin will be in the way of the backswing, thus stopping the coil.

The head is placed a little more to the right side than the left. The feeling of having it behind the ball is a good one.

When standing behind a good golfer looking down the target line, you see the arms hang away from the body.

Balance

The goal of every golfer should be to make a full swing that creates force *and stays in balance*. Balance in a golf swing is important. Counterbalance and a low center of gravity are needed in order to have balance. When you bend from the waist, there is a good chance you will not create a proper counterbalance in your posture or setup, so please bend from the hips!

When you stand to the ball correctly—that is, in balance—your head, shoulders, and upper chest are tilted forward. The total weight of these body parts is sizeable. Therefore, with this much body weight forward, there must be some body weight placed on the heels to counterbalance it.

When you use the short and mid-irons, the ball is placed just forward of center. This distance is even farther forward of this position when you use the longer clubs.

Try not to ground the club head because you cannot feel the weight of the club when it is on the ground. Just hold the club head an inch or so off the ground, and this will let you feel the weight that your inside is going to swing back and forth.

When you are standing to the ball, your chin is up, and there is an angle between the arms and club caused by the hands being low, not high. To create this all-important counterbalance in the setup, a golfer should bend from the hips, not the waist. This will ensure that the buttocks will move out slightly past the heels and create the required counterbalance.

Balance is also a result of a low center of gravity. A low center of grav-ity is as important to successful shot making as any element of the swing we could discuss. Reputable kinesiology professors agree that it has been scientifically proven that balance and a low center of gravity go hand in hand. In professional sports, the athletes who have outstanding balance or are difficult to knock off balance all retain low centers of gravity. Golfers who are able to keep balance throughout the swing have the proper setup, keep a low center of gravity. They swing without going up or down; they swing without changing the center of gravity.

The center of gravity for a golfer is located in the lower back. During the swing, this area should stay level. A quick start or change of direc-tion can contribute to a loss of balance. Some golfers make the mistake of putting the right hand on the club by reaching out and over the chest with the right arm and shoulder, which prevents the right shoulder from making a good coil. This puts another stop sign on the backswing (as does a chin that is too low). Put the right hand on the club *without* reach-ing across the chest. The feet, knees, hips, and shoulders are all pointing in the same direction, just left of or square to the target line.

Some very fine instructors like to have the shoulders pointing more to the left than the hips and feet. You may want to try this. These instruc-tors feel you can make a bigger natural coil from the shoulders pointing left at the start of the swing. I like golfers to feel that their arms are very light, not tight or heavy, and they should stay that way during the entire swing. The arms are *moved* backward and forward by the *inside*, and if they are tight or heavy, they cannot swing as they should.

Holding the Club

In my opinion, holding the club correctly is important, but it is not as complicated as some make it sound. First, I prefer the words *holding the club* rather than *gripping the club*. Gripping implies that strength must be applied, when that certainly should not be the case.

The club will be on the correct angle if it lies just under the heel pad of your left hand and across the pad of the carpal bone of the forefinger. To achieve this, simply hold the club in your left hand so that it crosses the lower palm of the hand while your fingers coil around the club.

With the right hand, the club is held mostly in the fingers. I prefer having learners use the *overlap* rather than the *interlock* style when holding the club. (It has been my experience that when a golfer joins the pinky of the right hand with the forefinger of the left, he holds on with these two fingers [interlocked] and will sometimes let go with the rest of his fingers during the swing.) A golfer's wrists should be light and flexible.

My suggestion is to place the pinky of the right hand over the forefinger of the left. Just lay it there, no pressure. There should be nine fingers on the club with this style, with the left thumb just right of center, and the right thumb just left of center. The palms face each other.

I know a lot has been written about how much pressure should be used when holding the club. I feel there should be no extra pressure with the thumb and forefinger. Just touch the club. When extra pressure is applied with these fingers, there is a tendency to stop the natural movements of the swing as well as the natural movements that occur in the wrist as the swing loads up going back and expands going forward. Extra pressure in the thumb and forefingers would be like several skaters in the middle of a skate line standing very rigid with the rest of the line's skaters relaxed. You can see how the skaters in the middle would take away from the natural movement and power of a skate line— and from the wrists of a golfer.

V's of grip (lines formed by the thumb and forefinger) point to the right side of the body.

The back of left hand and clubface are in line with each other, with a small natural inward bend in the left wrist.

The Club Becomes Longer

Over the years, many golfers with whom I have worked tell me they want to learn to hit down on the ball and take divots. From my point of view, divots are fine (the best swings produce thin divots), but *trying* to hit down will destroy the swing. You should only be trying to rotate. Yes, sound golf swings do take divots, but it's because rotation causes the arms and club to expand and become longer during the downswing than they were at address. With this added length, the swing then takes a divot automatically, without the golfer trying to hit down.

Explanation: At address, the end of the grip is a measurable distance from the ground. This distance is shorter than the club's actual length for two reasons:

1. At address the club is not placed at a perpendicular angle to the ground.
2. The club is designed so that the grip end falls forward of the club-head and ball at address.

Address

Fully extended

These two conditions and the natural actions of a sound swing are the reasons you should not be trying to hit down. As a sound swing is making ball contact, the club, arms, and wrist are about to become fully extended and stretched, and the right shoulder is lower than it was at address, all of which cause the club to become longer than it was at address, letting the swing take a divot.

The natural or automatic result of a sound swing is a club that becomes longer than it was at address (by at least 1 inch) and takes a divot after ball contact. There is no need to try to hit down in a sound golf swing. Expansion creates divots as the club becomes longer. Keep in mind that centrifugal force is also bending the club-head down. Studies show that it is only through impact that centrifugal force influences the swing and bends the toe of the club down.

Small Wheel

When the weight of the golf club stays back, wrist angle is retained, your swing will have what could be called a *small wheel*. In a factory that has conveyor belts, the belt that moves around a small wheel travels faster than a belt that moves around a larger wheel. When the wrist angle in your swing is retained (by the club staying back), it is similar to the small-wheel conveyor belt. Your hands and club travel around a small wheel before ball contact at top speed. When the wrist angle of your swing is not retained, it is similar to the big-wheel conveyor belt: Your hands and club are traveling around a large wheel before ball contact at a slower rate (see *opposite*).

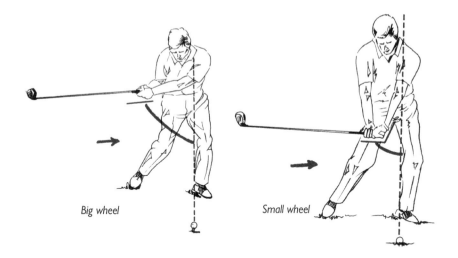

Big wheel   *Small wheel*

Mass—Velocity—Energy—Leverage

The energy of an object in motion is called *kinetic energy*. During a golf swing, kinetic energy has an effect on the club head. Energy is defined as "the ability to do work." The "work" of golf is the ability to compress the ball. This formula in physics is *MV*, or mass times velocity. It then follows that the greater the kinetic energy of the club head, the farther the ball goes.

Keep in mind that there are only two elements in this formula: mass (club head size and weight) and velocity (club head speed). That's all! Only mass and speed—no strength, power, or coil for tension. Once a golfer has the club in his or her hands, the mass cannot be changed—only the *speed* of the club head can be influenced during the swing. So how or what is the best way for a golfer to affect the speed of the club head so that it can achieve maximum force? The answer is *leverage*.

Physics tells us we can gain a mechanical advantage. In a sound golf swing this advantage will come from the law of leverage. This law states "force is multiplied by the length of the lever—the longer the lever, the greater the multiplier." For a golf swing to achieve its longest lever or the greatest multiplier that can accelerate the club to its greatest velocity, the force must be applied from a point as far away from the club head as possible.

A sound backswing has extension and width.

*When the **inside moves the outside,** you can see a space between the arms **(outside)** and the body **(inside)** at the start of a sound backswing that has width and extension. Soon the right arm starts to fold, and the wrists start to flex, creating two levers that expand during impact.*

The furthest distance from the club head is the center of the spine between the shoulders. This center becomes one of the pivot points of the swing for maximum multiplication (as in the laws of leverage).

When the swing comes from a rotating center, it has the ability to create maximum velocity in the downswing. The longer the lever, the greater the speed.

The backswing is affected by leverage. During the final stages of this part of the swing, the club slows down because the wrists have flexed and the right elbow has folded, causing the lever of the swing to shorten. This slows the club head naturally.

When golfers hit or cast from the top, they produce speed early in the downswing. If the wrists are not allowed to flex in the backswing, the lever of the swing stays extended too long, and the backward movement of the club head does not slow down to an acceptable change of direction speed, which can cause hitting or casting from the top.

When a golfer expands the lever of the swing early (too soon), there will be little or no natural velocity when the club head reaches the ball. Again, start your downswing with your right shoulder going down plane for maximum club head speed.

Trust Swinging the Weight of the Club

My suggestion to golfers is to just trust swinging back and forth. Do not try to hit the ball or be preoccupied with several swing thoughts. Learn the feel of a weight transfer and try to copy that feel every time you swing. Spend time learning the feel of your grip, stance, and the correct alignment of the club at impact. This is going to take time, so be prepared! You do not have to get overly involved in swing theory. When your *inside is moving your outside*, the laws of physics and math will help you create a sound swing.

A good example of the proper swinging weight transfer happens when a baseball player is warming up with a few swings of the bats. He is just turning his weight back and forth and the arms and bats are going along for the ride. The arms just seem to flow back and forth as the body moves them. This is how your swing should feel—light.

If you look closely at this baseball player warming up, watch how the bats are the last to come forward, moved by the swinging transfer of weight as the body turns forward. You may want to take two clubs and recreate the swinging movements of a baseball player. Make sure your arms are relaxed and light, and make no attempt to move them. Just turn back and forth, and the arms and clubs will be moved by the body turning its weight back and forth. This is as purely the *inside moving the outside* as happens in the golf swing or in other sports. Your swing will have extension, width, coil, stay on its plane, retain its angle, and have a balanced finish with the right side closer to the target than the left—when *the inside moves the outside*.

In a sound downswing, the hands and arms are also in the same position in a baseball swing.

Review

Your golf swing is very personal to you. It may have been developed with thoughts and ideas that were more involved than what I have given you here. To be sure, there is more than one way to learn a skill—any skill. The ideas and suggestions given here have taken years to develop and recognize. The end product is not a new way to swing a club, nor is it based on any new golf secrets. The information is sound and worthwhile, and it has helped professional and amateur golfers make progress.

When you toss a bean bag underhand to a target, it feels easier and smoother than when you throw a dart at a target. The reason is that the motion of the beanbag toss is a swinging transfer of weight, and a dart throw's motion is not.

On the other hand, a dart throw comes to a sudden stop, similar to the unsound golf swing, whereas the beanbag toss at its finish feels light and relaxed, similar to the sound golf swing. At the end of the beanbag toss, you cannot quite feel its finish—it is energy into nothingness. At the end of the dart throw, you can feel it come to a sudden stop, because it is a hand–wrist– lower arm movement that does not have a transfer of weight.

The beginner will not have very much to think about with this approach. The more advanced player will have a better understanding of what happens and why it happens in a sound golf swing. Finally, the expert golfers will develop a new trust in his or her swing.

When you trust *not* thinking about your hands and arms, golf will become less complicated. This will give you the opportunity to pay attention to playing and enjoying the game of golf. Thinking about the details of your swing is not necessary.

It has been my experience that when golfers begin to hit shots they are happy with and when they can recognize improvement, some become uncomfortable that they are not thinking about their hands and arms. It's just too simple! Then, when they hit a shot they are not happy with, they feel foolish. Such a simple thought—if it is true, why can't we do it all the time? Well, golf is not "all the time" for anyone—or for any approach.

Keep in mind that when we cannot do something that is or seems to be somewhat complicated, we will accept our lack of progress and keep working. But when information is given in a very simple way and we do not get the hang of it, it is only human nature to dismiss this simple thought or suggestion as incomplete or incorrect. Our egos will not admit that we have worked long enough with the suggestion. Again, it's only human nature to believe that things must be difficult to deserve to feel a sense of achievement.

The *inside-moves-the-outside* approach is very simple. It works—and it becomes more repeatable the more you work with it. Power in many sports is a swinging transfer of weight, and the *outside* (hands and arms) does not transfer very much weight—but the *inside* can.

Think about the way to throw a bowling ball or a frisbee. During the actions or movements of these acts, the only feeling you are aware of is motion and not any other details until the ball or frisbee is physically leaving your hand. At that time, you may be feeling power, or speed, or snap. The same is true in a sound golf swing. There is no feeling of extra speed or power during most of a sound golf swing. Golfers should be aware of their swinging motion, and only after the ball is on its way should there be a feeling of power or speed.

Progress and Becoming a Learner

We all have known golfers who play what could be called a steady game and others who truly do not know what to expect from one round of golf to the next. There are golfers who always seem to be improving their game and some who feel they will never see progress. Also, when we first start to play, some of us learn faster than others.

There are men and women who have been playing golf for years, spending a fair amount of money on lessons, equipment, green fees or dues, golf books, magazines, etc., and still see little or short-lived progress with their golf game. Are some golfers better athletes than others? Do some have better equipment? Are some stronger? I could go on, but perhaps the answer is that golfers who see faster and lasting progress have developed better learning skills.

After years of coaching and instructing golf at every level, I have the impression that some golfers do not know what to expect from the lesson experience. Few golfers understand what is involved in *learning* and, subsequently, making progress with their golf swing and game. These men and women may not know that the progress they would like to make is based largely on how they meet the responsibility of being a student or learner. Yes, there are students who do not know how to learn from a lesson; this should be no surprise. Remember, during our school years, very few of us made the progress we were capable of.

Years ago when the famous golf instructor, Tommy Armour, was asked to name golf's best instructor, he answered, "It takes great learners to make reputations for teachers." The instructor has a responsibility, but so does the student.

I honestly feel some students do not realize that if they want to see improvement, *they* must play a large part before, during, and after a lesson. Could some of the many lessons given every year in this country improve? Yes! Should some professionals improve what they do and how they do it? Yes! But this observation could—and does—go beyond professional golf into any and all professions (law, medicine, banking) and learning situations.

Here is my theory on approaching the lesson experience (before, during, *and* after): When you improve as a student, you improve as a golfer! You will understand more from the instruction you are receiving, whether it is from a book or a magazine or a lesson from a professional. The following sections of the book are designed to help you internalize this level of learning in your life. Remember: A master of anything was first a master of learning.

Before Your Lesson

First, before you take a lesson, it will help to understand that golf is an acquirable skill. Learning to golf is no different than learning to type, draw, or play a musical instrument. Like all acquirable skills, golf is learned in steps and stages. For some reason, however, when it comes to learning or improving our golf skills, the time it is surely going to take is overlooked.

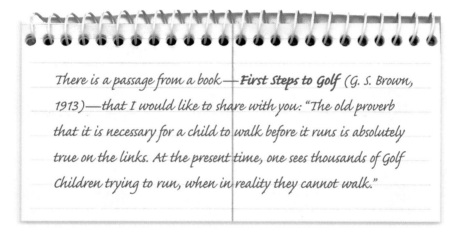

There is a passage from a book—***First Steps to Golf*** *(G. S. Brown, 1913)—that I would like to share with you: "The old proverb that it is necessary for a child to walk before it runs is absolutely true on the links. At the present time, one sees thousands of Golf Children trying to run, when in reality they cannot walk."*

Before going to your appointment for instruction, you should realize it is just that: a session of *instruction*. It is not a test. Some golfers try very hard to make a good impression on their instructor. Please do not be concerned about how you are going to look to your instructor. You are not going to embarrass yourself. Relax and be yourself, and the lesson will go just fine. Remember…this is not a test! See instructors as learning partners, not as evaluators of poor outcomes.

Before getting started with lessons, it helps to know that any progress a student is going to make is because of the investment of time *they* are willing to make. It is the teamwork between you and your instructor that produces the results that both are looking for. Students must also work on their own. Instructors can impart core knowledge, but skill must be developed by the student's personal experiences.

Golf is a game of control based on self-control. As you start to learn and gain experience, remember: This alone will not lead to progress. It is what you do with the knowledge and experience you have gained that leads to the progress you are looking for in your game. *Focus on what you want to do, not on fixing poor habits. Focus on what the golf club should do for the shot you are about to play and not on any details concerning your body segments.*

Next, before you even make an appointment for your lesson, gather some information about the instructor. Some professionals give a large volume of lessons, and this can be an indication of their skill. Find out if this instructor is teaching a wide range of golfers—men and women and high and low handicappers. The approach to instruction should vary with each student.

A good source for obtaining the name of a qualified instructor is other golfers. You may see or play with someone whose game you like; ask where they have taken lessons. If you feel the golf staff at the club or course where you play most of your golf are not the ones to help you with your game, ask them to make a suggestion as to who you could make an appointment with. Take the time to find an instructor you feel is going to take a real interest in you and your golf game.

My final "before" suggestion: There is a chance you will feel that you are not improving—or perhaps even regressing after taking lessons. This is only natural. But if you are aware of this beforehand, you have started to understand the whole learning and lesson experience.

During Your Lesson

Be early for your lessons, and use the time while you wait to start your lesson warmup. When first meeting with your instructor, I suggest you tell him or her what you would like to work on during your time together. At times, you may suggest one area only to have the instructor suggest you should work in a different area first. Do not try to guide or take over the lesson—let the instructor do his or her job.

For instance, maybe you want to work on your backswing but your instructor wants to talk about something else. **Let the instructor do the guiding!** Remember, golf is learned in steps and stages. Ask the instructor to explain the what and why of his suggestions. Sometimes, when trying to be polite to a student, the instructor backs off the direction in which he or she may have taken the lesson. As the student, if you do not let this happen, your lesson will be more effective.

There are times when we have decided to take a lesson and expect the instructor will want us to make a big change in our style. Our game is way off, and we feel it is going to take a big change to bring our game around to familiar standards. Often, however, this is not the case. Keep in mind that the swing you make is, for the most part, based on your grip, stance, posture, alignment, and balance. So even though your game is way off its normal level, it may be only a small suggestion about fundamentals that will bring your game back.

A new golfer may understand the required movements of a sound golf swing for a long time before he advances enough to also implement a sound grip, proper stance and balance, and correct alignment. Both the new and experienced golfers should be prepared to spend time learning these fundamentals.

When an instructor asks his students what they would like to work on, the most common answer is, "I can hit my irons, but my woods give me trouble." Please understand: The swing is the same for both woods and irons. After watching a few swings with each type of club, my instructor's eye will see the same mistake. The only difference is that with the shorter iron clubs, the mistake is smaller than with the larger wood clubs. Students are misled by the shot with an iron that went only 6 yards left or right and still hits the green—what they don't realize is that the same swing with the wood would have produced a shot that was 15 or 20 yards off line. So "Let's work on the woods" is the student's suggestion. But don't be too unhappy if your instructor instead wants to work on the fundamentals of the golf swing—stance, alignment, and balance—because he or she is heading you in the right direction.

When making swings during your lesson, it may be helpful to understand that because you cannot see yourself swing, you are making a swing that is different than the one you believe you are making. We can also be misled by what we are feeling while making a swing.

If you see some progress during your lesson, this is great. But do not be disappointed if you do not. The suggestions in a lesson may take some time for your own style and feel to adjust to them. When working with a new suggestion, never—and I mean *never*—say to yourself, "This feels funny or awkward." This would plant a negative thought. Instead, just say, "Well this feels new, and I will give myself some time," or "When I have more experience, I will do this better."

During a lesson, ask questions and take notes. Have your instructor give you several different word pictures of what to do. When you have more than one way or thought to make something happen in the swing, you will add an element to your game that can only help. Your body cannot teach you a thing—only the mind can. You may hit some very nice shots while taking a lesson, but you may feel this will not happen on the course. This is sometimes true, but after more practice you will be able to bring your practice-range swing onto the golf course.

During the lesson, your instructor will probably want to make only one or two suggestions. Do not feel short-changed. We can only practice one part of the swing at a time; more than that and the lesson would be less helpful. At the completion of your lesson, ask what questions you would like, and then find out when your instructor would like to see you again.

Percy Boomer told us, "Habit, good or bad, in golf or outside of it, needs time to consolidate."

When working on your golf game, please do not forget about the short game. Pitching, chipping, and putting make up over 60% of the swings we make in a round of golf. Short-game instruction may be more helpful in lowering your score than long-game instruction. I suggest that you practice the short game three hours for every hour of long-game practice.

After Your Lesson

What students do after a lesson will make a difference in the type of progress they will see. It is important to have a clear understanding of the suggestions your instructor made about your style. But it is what you do with those suggestions that will make a difference in your game. I would not suggest going out to play a round of golf immediately after a lesson. Suggestions made in a lesson must be worked on for a while on a practice range. The lesson is what you take away—it's not the time you spend with the instructor.

Let's look at the round of golf that the score of 100 is made. You are on the course for 4 to 4.5 hours, and take 2 putts per hole. That leaves 64 shots, of which let's say 14 are chip or short shots around the green. This would leave 50 full swings. Fifty full swings equals one pail of balls at a practice range, which takes 20–30 minutes to hit. In fact, because each ball takes only a few seconds to put in place and hit, you could say that 50 full swings is really only about 3 or 4 minutes actually of swing time. You have been on the course for hours, but have only minutes of swing time to show for it. Can you imagine only practicing typing for minutes each week? Progress would be very slow.

Therefore, our suggestion to any golfer—whether you are working on a new suggestion or trying to keep your game in shape—is to always have more swing time off the course than on. A few hours of practice time is like playing several rounds of golf. When you are playing golf, tips from other players are as free as the rain from the sky. *Please* do not be a willing target for them. Friends mean well, but they are going to slow the learning process. You will drown in well-meaning suggestions. At the practice range or on the course, your main challenge will be to keep using the suggestions your instructor has made, even when you are hitting poor shots—to not try to fix it but rather focus on what to *do*. Poor shots are part of the learning process. Poor shots should be seen as feedback, not as failure. It's like misspelling a word. Remember that is how we learned to spell—from the feedback of misspelling.

There is a point where golf is really a self-taught game. We need an instructor to show us what we should be working on—but when we start to practice and pay attention and remember the outcome of our actions, we are actually teaching ourselves the game of golf. In a sense, instructors cannot *teach* you, but they can help you *learn*. This is the cornerstone of the after-lesson segment of the lesson experience. We are teaching ourselves when we practice correctly. Keep in mind that any and all golfers, at every level, experience ups and downs throughout their personal golfing history. Understand that your golf game will always be hot and cold. Your challenge is to bring the two natural extremes together more often than not. Also, learn that some days are better than others.

When on the course playing, do just that—play golf. Do not get overly involved with swing theory. Pay attention to your alignment and then swing. Save the theory for the practice range; on the course, just play golf. Ask your instructor for tips on taking your game and style to the course.

When on a practice range take your time between swings. Do not hit ball after ball quickly. Take your time. Think about the suggestion you and your instructor are working on. Always hit to a target—this is a must if your practice is to be useful.

I feel that most golfers fail to reach their potential—not due to a lack of talent as golfers but to their inability to be a good student, which can often hold golfers back. We could say that golf swings do not hit bad shots—mind sets and fear of failure do. I hope the suggestions made here will help your understanding of the lesson experience. I truly feel most golfers can reach their potential when they improve as students of the game.

Part III

Research

As part of this 2007 revised edition, I would like to point out that with the world of high-speed digital cameras and related editing equipment, we have a great deal more information about the golf swing today than could have been concluded using earlier research techniques. For historical purposes, I decided to leave this research section as it originally appeared.

During the 1980s, scientifically structured research tests were conducted at Centinela Medical Center's Biomechanics Lab (Inglewood, California). The purpose of the particular research I am referring to was to analyze and identify which muscles were being used and when during a golf swing.

The research findings of the study of which muscles were being used and when during a golf swing are as follows:

A. Both the left and right sides of the body play equal roles in providing power for the swing. The researchers felt these findings might surprise some golf instructors who feel (for right handed golfers) golf is a left-sided game. Tests do show there is equal emphasis (regardless of being a right or left handed golfer) from both sides of the body during the swing.

B. Less skilled players tend to get less than half the trunk rotation of a skilled player. The most noticeable difference seen on film when comparing amateurs to professionals is their lack of trunk rotation. Research showed without trunk rotation there is a loss of motion which enables the body segments to transmit maximum velocity to the club head at impact.

Golfers give themselves a noticeable handicap by letting their available arc of motion diminish through lack of flexibility and by failing to realize the importance of Body Rotation. Power in a golf swing can be achieved by rotating the body segments through space, and transferring energy from one segment to the next. When you diminish the space through which these segments move, then you must use more muscle power or effort to derive the same output.

In the academic world, they are called *prerequisites*—classes that must be taken before you can go ahead to the next subject. I feel golf has some prerequisites. Greater enjoyment and progress will come to the golfer who not only has some insights into golf techniques but also some understanding of golf's prerequisites.

There is more to playing golf than hitting the ball. You need to be aware of these prerequisites before progress can come. In fact, the earlier in your golfing career, the better! For readers who have been playing for some time, being aware of golf's prerequisites will help you to better understand your past golfing experiences. For a new golfer, your efforts to improve will be more productive.

Progress and enjoyment from golf will be aided when we realize that being discouraged and golfing go hand in hand. When you are discouraged, you play golf asking yourself such questions as "How long will it take to learn?", "How many lessons will it take?", "How can I play the front nine so well and the back nine so poorly?", and "Why am I good one day and bad the next?" These are the questions discouraged golfers ask.

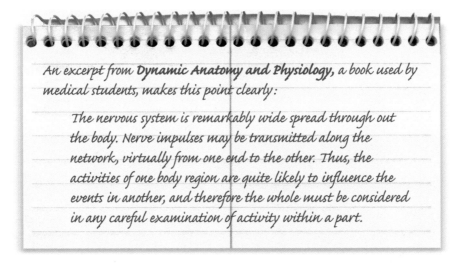

An excerpt from **Dynamic Anatomy and Physiology**, a book used by medical students, makes this point clearly:

> The nervous system is remarkably wide spread through out the body. Nerve impulses may be transmitted along the network, virtually from one end to the other. Thus, the activities of one body region are quite likely to influence the events in another, and therefore the whole must be considered in any careful examination of activity within a part.

The only thing constant about golf is its inconsistency! A fact for Tiger Woods; a fact for me; a fact for you. No one plays well all the time, nor do we fulfill our potential in every round. Any golfer, professional or amateur, will experience their game coming and going in a round of golf. It's the nature of the game.

If you have prepared yourself for the natural ups and downs of golf, you will have made a big step in understanding the game. Golf is not like a column of figures that are absolute and can be added up correctly every time. When you fully recognize that both the new and experienced golfers have bad days, or bad weeks, or bad months, it will then be easier to break out of your own slump.

Your progress in golf is normally directly related to the amount of time you spend on your game. If your schedule does not permit much time for golf, your progress will tend to be slower than someone who has more time.

Even when you are spending what you feel is a lot of time and work on your golf game, the progress may be slower than you think it should be. Let me try to help you understand what spending lots of time on your game means.

Ask a golfer how long they have been playing golf and you may get an answer of 5, 10, or upwards of 15 years, followed by followed by such comments as "and I *still* don't break 100."

Let's examine the 5-year golfer. Suppose he plays an average of twice a week for 10 months of the year. That will be 80 times a year or 400 times over 5 years. The average score has been 115, with 36 putts per round. That would give us a total number of 31,600 golf swings (less putts) over 5 years.

These 31,600 golf swings do *not* equal 5 years of golfing. For 1 year, it would be 100 swings a day with 49 days off. That is less than a tournament professional (and some amateurs) plays in a year and about 2 years of golf for some serious golfers.

We must realize that most of us are part-time golfers. When you try to improve your game in terms of quality, it's a must that you keep in mind that you are not a professional. This will help your progress without making you discouraged. If one of your goals is to improve, practice may become more important to you. For sure, ***progress will yield to practice***. Golfers who play well have worked on their game.

Your Nervous System and Golf

Playing golf when you are nervous is something all good golfers have learned to do. To make progress in this area, it may help to first learn a little about our nervous system and then be aware that successful golf is more than paying attention at the first tee.

Your nervous system (emotions) will have a greater effect on your golf than a good set of clubs, top-grade balls, or a lesson from the instructor. The effect will either be positive or negative. Before every swing, as you prepare to play your next shot, the nervous system will play a major part in the result.

Controlling or having a consistent golf game is the equivalent of controlling or having consistent emotions. Small or distant distractions can be as damaging as closer and larger ones. It may take some work on your part, but the results will be worth the effort. You are capable of being in a state of grace, ready to make smooth, gracefully rhythmic swings.

   FACT: You need to slow down, take your time, and pace yourself! Start your mental preparation long before you even get to the golf course so that you will be in your "state of grace" when you step up to the first tee. When you rush to the course feeling stressed, you can be assured that you will not play up to the level that you play when you are swinging in your cool, calm, and collected state of grace.

For some players, preparation for a round of golf should start the night before. Other golfers may find enough time when they first get up in the morning. The medical profession knows that what we do in one part of our body, or life will have an effect on other parts. Successful golfers must educate themselves on the best way of working with their own nervous systems.

At times, events away from the course can affect our play. I have seen golfers who have gone through a change in their lives (death of a family member, divorce, money problems, etc.) and, either after or during these times, their golf performance does not reach the level they were once familiar with.

Most golfers go to the course to enjoy the day and have a good time. So go and enjoy; approach a day of golf in the same manner you approach other days in your life when the sole purpose is to enjoy yourself.

Okay, let's go; we can relax and have a good time. The key word is *relax*.

State of Grace

Some say that golf is a game played in the state of grace. I believe that graceful is the way most good players feel. There is sometimes an exception, but most good golfers feel at ease. They feel smoothness. They all worked on trying to achieve this state of grace, some more than others. Good players all walk at a pace that helps them stay at ease. Some good players have gone as far as to change their way of life, their way of talking, and where they live. Some have become more involved with religion. All this has been done to gain the inner peace that sometimes manifests itself in a golf swing that is in the state of grace.

If you start off by leaving on time for the course, you will not have to run from your car to the first tee. You will have time for a warmup. Hit some practice balls. Practice a little putting. Before you start the round, a warmup is a must. You will not play to your capability unless you warm up to get your touch and feel going. If a practice area is not available, do a few exercises to warm up your body.

On the course, remember to keep in touch with the pace of your game. Try not to make any real quick movements. Do not yell or get excited. Do not grab clubs from your bag. Take them out slowly. Do not run to the next tee. Walk. Try not to get overly excited about a good shot or very angry about the poor ones. *Be in control of your emotional system.* Remember, what you're doing with one part of your body will have an effect on other parts. Golf is a game played in the state of grace not only from the start of your round but also for several hours before. You cannot let your nervous system get overly involved with what you are trying to do in golf. Pick the club that you feel can get the job done. Then address the ball in a relaxed manner and swing. Do not start thinking about any trouble your shot could get you into. Likewise, you cannot let your body get all keyed up trying to make a birdie. Stay calm and keep it simple, and you will hit more good shots than ever before.

After the shot has been played, the same approach must be maintained. Do not get worked up over bad shots. Find the ball, and try to do your best with the next swing. Be "in the now"; keep your mind on what you are doing. Remember the feel of your good swings and repeat that feel. A good shot can also get a golfer emotionally worked up. Try not to let this happen. Keep your mind on what you are doing. When you have more control over your nervous system, you have more control of your golf game. Keep yourself in the state of grace. Smooth and easy does it.

 The next time you watch a professional tournament, be aware of the shot-by-shot emotional response of the players, and note their concentration and regrouping techniques.

Imaging—It May Be the Secret

*The word **think** is defined in the following way: "To form or conceive in the mind; to have in mind an idea, image, conception; to analyze or examine; to bear in mind; to recollect or remember; to form a plan." And this is only part of the long definition that appears in most dictionaries.*

We can postulate from this that *imaging* is one way to define *thinking*. But have we discovered the secret of good golf when we refer to imaging? Well, it could be that imaging belongs high on the list of essentials for good golf. It is certain that you cannot learn or play golf without the imaging process.

Physical actions occur after a *mental* message has been sent from our brain to our body. A golfer often will credit a good round to his mental approach or the way he or she was thinking. A champion golfer once said, "I have found that success on the course depends on the way you think." Another champion said, "The mind always has to operate before the muscles go to work, and the muscles must only operate once the mind is working."

For our purposes, we'll talk about four parts of the imaging process (that is, right brain-hemisphere functions) that come into play most frequently for a good golfer. These are *concentration*, *recollection*, *imagination*, and *anticipation*.

Concentration　Golf will always be more of a mental challenge than a test of your physical skill. You must *focus on what you are doing* when playing, practicing, taking a lesson, or reading a book on golf. Try to think only about playing golf.

Concentration starts with positive thoughts, both on the course and when practicing. Think about one shot at a time on the course. Do not let your mind replay past shots that were poor. Fear of trouble will break your concentration. Take your time. Do not rush into your swing. Picture what you are trying to do. Wind, distance, uphill or downhill, and other factors should be taken into consideration subconsciously before every shot.

Again, when practicing, take your time between swings. When you are taking a useful approach to your practice session, a small bucket of balls will last half an hour or sometimes even longer. Focus simply and picture your swing. Trying to think about several parts at the same time will slow down the progress.

Recollection Some golfers can tell you, shot for shot, about a round of golf they played several years ago. If you tend to forget things about your golf that might be helpful in the future, it's time to change. It is very helpful to remember things about the course you are playing: fast greens, traps you cannot see, uphill and downhill lies, etc. This can be accomplished by *staying in the present* when you are playing a round of golf.

If you cannot recall the speed of greens (to keep your touch or feel from hole to hole); if you cannot remember how far you can hit using a particular club; if you cannot remember distances; if you cannot recall what your shot will do in the wind; if you cannot recall the feel of your good swings—then you are making golf harder than it should be, and more than likely have been overly concerned with the results of your actions.

One of the most important uses of recollection comes when you try to repeat a shot you hit a few holes ago or last week. If you cannot remember what the swing felt like, your chances of duplicating that shot are very low.

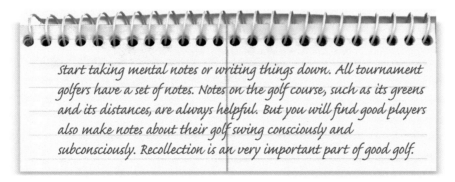

start taking mental notes or writing things down. All tournament golfers have a set of notes. Notes on the golf course, such as its greens and its distances, are always helpful. But you will find good players also make notes about their golf swing consciously and subconsciously. Recollection is an very important part of good golf.

Imagination Imagination is a mental tool that is always useful, especially when we have hit the ball into trouble.

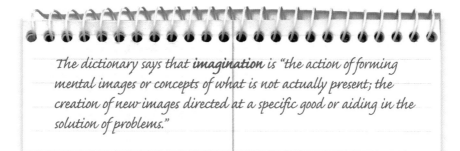

*The dictionary says that **imagination** is "the action of forming mental images or concepts of what is not actually present; the creation of new images directed at a specific good or aiding in the solution of problems."*

Every golfer finds trouble from time to time, but some seem to handle it better than others. At times, you have to make up a shot or a swing. The ball is in a spot that no orthodox approach would of use. First, you should be just trying to get the ball back to a place where your normal swing can be used. To do this is likely going to take a little imagination. You may have to turn the clubface over, or you may have to stand on one foot, or you may have to hold the club one-handed. You may have to swing backwards! Any of a number of approaches can be helpful at times. When practicing, I will sometimes make up shots and try different stances so they will not be entirely new when I try them on the course.

Most common trouble shots involve a ball that finds its way under a tree into a spot that gives you little or no chance to make a full swing. Get down on your knees and swing the club around yourself like a baseball bat. You now will be able to make ball contact and get the ball out of trouble. Always be thinking, and let your natural imagination help with some of those shots that look impossible. A good working knowledge of the options available through the rules of golf can also get you out of trouble with the least number of strokes.

Anticipation The mental choices you make before your swing will affect the outcome of the shot more than the swing. You must be on guard *not* to antici-pate hitting a shot you have not been successful with before.

Play within yourself. Do not try to win with one swing. Golfers who anticipate the bounce or roll of a shot beforehand are increasing their chances of a good result. A warning: Anticipating the results is very helpful, but don't be unrealistic. The golfer who anticipates a result that would be far beyond his normal capabilities is only asking for trouble. Playing within your capabilities is the key to good golf. The winner is the player who makes the fewest mistakes.

Watch—Learn—and Mimic

Watching good golfers and mimicking what they do can be an effective way to improve your own golf. Most of what we learned as children came from mimicking others. So why not apply that thought to golf? My suggestion is to watch professional golfers playing in tournaments. Watch and mentally record their warmup practice if you can, and play your recording back at slower speeds to see their swings. *Warning!* Please don't try to copy *exactly* what professional golfers do, but rather take away a general impression to mimic.

When you watch all these good players, your first observation will be that they all look different. Different swings, different sizes. So how can you learn anything? Believe me, if you know what to look for, there is a lot to be gained from mimicking good players.

Yes, they all look different—when you don't know what to look for. But when you are looking at some of the fundamentals that exist in all good golfers, they start to look more alike.

*A list of observations you should make when watching good players includes **posture, grip, head placement, leg work,** the **complete backswing,** the **swing down,** and the **routine before the swing.***

Posture   Observe and mimic how a good player's posture does not change very much from club to club. The only real change is that as the club gets longer, the player is standing farther away from the ball and the feet get wider. The arms are the same from the elbow up as they lay on the chest, and the shoulders are still the same with the right lower than the left. The back is in the same position. Good players have a small bend from the hips, and their buttocks are out just a little with a slight bend at the knees. Please note the overall lack of tension!

Grip   Observe and copy how good players do *not* look as though they are holding on to the club for dear life. Their swings have rhythm. If they were holding the club with tight wrists, they would not have any rhythm. Professional players are very smooth when they do anything with the club.

Head Placement   Observe and copy where a good player places his head. Draw an imaginary line from the left ear down to the ground. You will find that at the start of their swing many good players have their head placed in back of the ball (with the tee shot especially). They will keep their head back throughout the swing until the ball is hit.

Leg Work   Observe and mimic the leg action of good players. Most poor golfers have no leg or foot work in their style. So watch how a good golfer's legs are a part of the backswing and downswing. Every good golfer has his legs working during the entire swing. The legs are shifting weight back and forth in response to swinging the club.

Complete Backswing   Observe and mimic how good players turn and swing, transferring the weight. Poor golfers hardly ever transfer weight in the backswing. Look at the turns of good players—club, hands, arms, and shoulders move as a unit. This helps your swing have the smoothness and power needed to play consistent golf.

Swing Down   Observe and mimic a good player's swing as it starts down; it does not pick up a great deal of speed. The start of the downward swing is smooth—just as smooth as the start of the backswing. Good players are not trying to add anything extra to the start of the downswing. When a poor golfer starts down, most times it involves quick movement without rhythmic grace. "It may help to see the swing as having a start and a finish with nothing between. Just swing the weight of the club." (Susan Berdoy Meyers)

Routine Before the Swing Observe and mimic how all good players go through the same subconscious pattern of movement before every swing. Consistent golf starts subconsciously with a consistent routine before every shot. Good players believe that this repeated pattern of movements adds a repeated pattern to their shots. Every player has a little different routine, but before every shot, the same subconscious pattern of movements is repeated. The next time you watch a good player, look for the fundamentals that all good players have in common and mimic them. Good golfers have different styles, but they all have fundamentals that are very similar. Your game will improve when your fundamentals improve.

Control

Golf is a game of influencing distance and direction. The better players do hit bad shots, but there is little difference between the results of the bad shots and the good shots. Professionals have control built on a few fundamentals. Golf, when played well, is not a game made up of only great shots, but a game void of bad shots. Remember, a golf course is made up of 150 acres and has 18 different holes played with 14 clubs but with only two types of shots: the long shots and the short shots. It is important that you keep in mind that golf is a *target* game. Short-game thinking while you are playing the long game is sometimes very helpful. No one ever walks onto the green without looking for the hole or the best line to the hole. So when walking down the fairway or onto the tee, find a target to keep in mind.

It's Different

There is a big difference between golf and other sports we play. Tennis, baseball, basketball, football, etc., are sports in which most of the player's movements are *reactive,* or controlled and caused by the opponent. In tennis, for example, if the ball goes that-a-way, so must you. And so it is in other sports. But in golf—which is started from a standing still position and the movement is self-imposed—you do not have anyone causing you to move one way or the other. You are on your own. You are not reacting to a ball or another person. You have to create a movement. This makes golf a creative endeavor. The golfer is very much like a solo actor or actress who walks out onto the stage and then begins to perform. The actor's movements are self-created and not a reaction to someone else's dialogue or movement.

Because the movements of the golf swing are created, any and all elements of being a performer hold true. In my approach to golf instruction, a lot of time is spent in this area. Trying to help a golfer improve is much like trying to help an actor become a better performer.

In other sports where movements are controlled by those with whom we are playing, we are always reacting to the movement of others. In golf, we focus on each shot being played. If you shot 95, it was not one game but 95 different performances—95 different times your brain had to tell your body what to do. Before each shot, the golfer must "call a play" so the swing will know what to do.

Approaches that are less threatening can be used when the new golfer can see the game of golf as a non-judged performance. Many players feel as though everyone is looking at them when they are on the first tee. Avoid all the old self-conscious scripts and focus on allowing yourself to *feel* the swing. *Then swing without concern for the outcome.*

It is not unusual for new golfers to slow their own progress by trying to hit every shot perfectly. As you become more seasoned, you will adapt to taking the bad with the good, putting the less desirable behind you. Experienced performers are aware that we humans can never do something exactly the same way every time, and they are prepared to keep going and move past a less-than-desirable performance.

Split Eyes and Mind

Look at the ball, but feel or visualize something else. Lots of golfers find themselves looking at the ball and also thinking about it. You cannot play golf and think about the ball.

When you drive a car, you look at the road with your eyes, but you can simultaneously think about or feel almost anything at the same time. We can multitask on the phone as well, looking and observing something around us while talking to the person on the phone. We should use this ability to split our eyes and mind when we play golf. Look at the ball but visualize what you are going to do or feel in your swing. Learn to look at the ball and feel something else.

It's in the Middle

Recognize that the golf swing has little to do with the ball. A golf ball is at the halfway point of the swing, not at the end of the swing. The ball is in the middle. When good players make a practice swing, they are trying to feel the swing and they are often trying to repeat the feel of the last shot they were happy with. Also, the practice swing of a good player looks very much like their swing when playing. Again, they are trying to repeat the feel of their swing.

As you read on, let's point out again that golfers can very easily be misled by what we think we see and think we feel. Very easily! When golfers say they can see or feel roll, they are being tricked or misled by their eyes and feel. Also, if feel has not been tied correctly to a picture or visualization, it will always be misleading.

Before explaining what happens to the hands and wrists during the downswing, it would help if you understand that in a sound swing, the wrists are very flexible (sometimes called *oily*). Because of this flexibility, the weight of the club head and rotational force causes wrists to bend or flex into different alignments as the swing is in motion. They are not being consciously bent.

*The first step in understanding what happens to the hands and wrists during the swing is to look at the position they take during the address. Note how the right hand has been placed on top or over the left hand. Also note that the lower part of the right arm is level with or below the left arm, and there is no forward, backward, up, or down bend in the wrists. Let's call this position **center**, or **on plane**. Your hands are going to stay in this address position throughout the swing (right and on top with no bends) until the weight of the club head causes this relationship to be altered under the laws of motion.*

- Findings show that it's the large muscles in the body that supply most of the power in a golf swing. A muscle's power is in proportion to its cross-sectional area or size; meaning that the bigger it is, the more potential power it has.

- Tests also show that less skilled golfers tend to swing the club primarily with the arms, while failing to use the power available to them in their trunk, hips and legs. The golfer who is a hands-and-arms swinger loses a tremendous amount of potential power by failing to get a good body turn that makes use of the larger muscles.

- When test results compared professionals with amateurs, the results showed skilled players use a much lower percentage of their muscular power in their swing. When the whole body is rotating, swinging the club takes less muscular effort. This is consistent with what the Biomechanics Lab has learned while investigating other sports such as tennis and basketball.

This research has given the sports world a keen appreciation for the contributions made by the trunk and the lower body as it relates to what happens at impact. The research results encourage all golfers (and other related sports players) to emphasize these parts of the body instead of only arms, hands and wrists.

The following research tests were done by the Golf Society of Great Britain in the early 1960s. The complete findings can be found in the book *The Search For The Perfect Swing*, a book that belongs in every golf enthusiast's library.

Power—A good golfer can generate up to 4 horsepower. This is surprisingly high power—and it leaves no doubt that the big muscles of the legs and trunk play a greater part in the top class players striking of the ball than those of his arms and hands.

Force—The force applied to the ball by the club head during impact in a full drive rises to a peak of about 2,000 pounds—with an average of 1,400 pounds.

Feel—When a golfer's brain can be said to have felt the impact of a shot the ball is already 15 yards away. It takes two-thirds of a millisecond for the shock of impact to travel up the shaft from the clubface to the hands and the ball is already in flight about .5" clear of the clubface. At least a further ten milliseconds elapses before the message gets to the golfer's brain. It would be at least another fifth of a second before orders from the golfer's brain could cause his hands to take any action to modify the stroke, and nothing can be done to affect the ball, which by this time would be 15 yards away.

Speed—The top class of golfers may accelerate the club head about one hundred times as fast as the fastest sports car can accelerate (1960s): From the top of the backswing to over 100 miles per hour at impact; all in as little as one fifth of a second. Traveling at 100 miles per hour, a driver head sends the ball away at about 135 miles per hour.

Off Line Shots—Pulls and pushes are straight shots in the wrong direction. For every 1° the swing itself is off line—the push or pull will be 3.5 yards from the intended line, on a 200-yard shot. A shot that is 21 yards off line, the direction of the swing must be 6° off line—quite a big error of swing. Hooks and slices are caused by the clubface aiming, at impact, in a different direction from the line in which the club head is being swung. These shots will go twice as far off line as pulls or pushes. The clubface that points only 1° off the direction in which it is swung, will send the ball 7 or 8 yards off line. The 21 yards off line shot needs less than a 3° mistake in face alignment.

What these scientific facts mean in plain language is that *what we all feel is not how we are hitting the ball, but how we have already hit it.* This means that when hitting a drive, the player, in effect, puts his club head into orbit at more than 100 miles per hour around himself and—because he can't do anything else—*perforce* leaves the club head to hit the ball entirely on its own, in the path and at the speed the golfer has already given it.

For all the effect we can have on it, the club head at the moment of impact might just as well be connected to our hands by a number of strings holding it to the circle of its orbit. Any top-class player's swing consistently manages to align his or her clubface at impact within 2° of the direction of their swing. That is pretty narrow bounds within which to confine natural human errors for a full-length shot. To achieve this accuracy, the swing has to be as simple as possible.

An efficient swing must have speed, accuracy, and the ability to repeat itself consistently. All possible sources of human error that cause variations from swing to swing must be reduced to a minimum, therefore, avoiding any very complicated forms of movements. **To repeat itself consistently, the swing must use the fewest moving parts!**

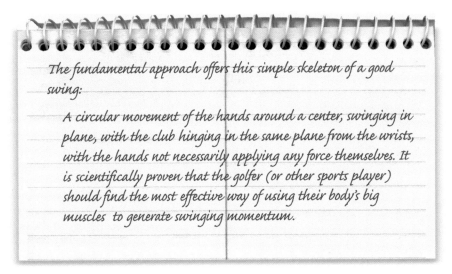

The fundamental approach offers this simple skeleton of a good swing:

A circular movement of the hands around a center, swinging in plane, with the club hinging in the same plane from the wrists, with the hands not necessarily applying any force themselves. It is scientifically proven that the golfer (or other sports player) should find the most effective way of using their body's big muscles to generate swinging momentum.

Difficulties in Maintaining Plane

Some studies show that there are one or two specific points in the swing where things can very easily swing out of alignment or off plane: the takeaway and the first movement of the downswing.

The club head's momentum on the backswing will have tended to take the club head back on whatever path the takeaway started it on.

One very important thing to realize about the downswing, once the swing has gotten properly underway it will tend to follow the plane it was set off in.

Scientists feel it can help a golfer to have in his mind a clear uncomplicated picture of the basic movements he or she is using that can govern all the complications of limbs, muscles and joints. This is where the idea of the whole swing working around a central hub may be very useful to golfers. The idea of a hub governing the swing from somewhere between the shoulders can make an excellent practical basis for trying to swing the club on plane.

Tests show that although the actual movements taking place at the joints a golfer uses are quite complicated but the constant overall tendency will be for a swinging action itself to smooth out the complications of its own accord. The swinging momentum of a golf club will try to move in the smoothest and simplest possible way. We do not, in any way, have to force the swing. On the contrary, the art of golf lies in allowing our swing to happen.

Natural Swing Findings

Scientists found that the structural movements the golfer makes during a sound swing will look quite complicated if taken bit by bit. The movements we need to make in order to reproduce a sound swing are really unexpectedly few and simple.

Scientists have broken the backswing down into five movements:

1. *Turning of upper chest*
2. *Swinging the arms*
3. *Wrist cocking*
4. *Club moving on plane*
5. *The arms and hands move together*

Scientists found describing these movements much more complicated than carrying them out. They happen quite naturally if they are given the chance to. It seems certain that the correct top-of-backswing position is the successful coordination of the first foot or so of the swing. If this is achieved, the rest of the backswing will tend to follow naturally.

When this is not achieved, or if any other moves are deliberately or excessively used at this stage, the whole backswing is likely to be made much more difficult to complete correctly. This is why some professionals often advise a one-piece-take-away or all-together-swing.

Downswing Findings

To investigate the workings of the swing scientifically, a team of research scientists fed information into a computer to carry out experiments in terms of mathematics alone. What the team found was the sequence of movements in the downswing is really much simpler than in the backswing.

There is never any unnecessary slack. From the body to the club head everything happened or should happen in a tight sequence. The general conclusion holds: That every part of the rotating and swinging system must be pulled around until that part can no longer apply useful work. In terms of a human golfer, the trunk and the shoulders pull the arms, the arms the hands, the hands the shaft, and the shaft the club head. The primary power for the sound swing is going to start in sequence from the trunk and big muscles of the chest and back.

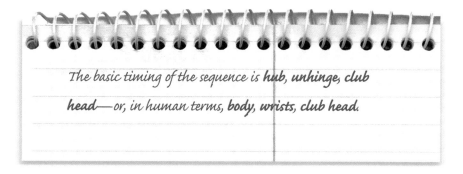

The basic timing of the sequence is **hub, unhinge, club head**—*or, in human terms,* **body, wrists, club head.**

Through the Ball

Research findings show that *in order to reproduce the actions through the ball that fit into the requirements of a sound swing, the golfer does the following things*:

> *Start the upper lever down and through the swing in plane.* It is the hub and shoulder action that sets the plane, pattern and timing of swinging at the golf ball. Thus, during the first stage, before the club head has been given enough momentum to follow the plane set for it in the downswing, the shoulder action must work in a way that gets the whole action moving in the plane required. Doing this may be difficult because of the tendency for the right arm and side (right-handed player), to take over control too soon. I suggest just swinging the weight of the club through impact by letting *the inside move the outside*!

Follow-through

The follow-through is an inevitable continuation of the swinging action through the ball. It serves the purpose of absorbing the momentum of the body, arms and club left over after impact. The primary force during the follow-through will be, of course, the momentum in the club head itself. The aim of the swing is to transfer as much as possible, the momentum generated in the body and arms out into the club head at impact. So much momentum is absorbed by the club head that the club head now is pulling the swing into its follow-through against the resistance of the arms, body and legs.

How Muscles Work in Golf

The main power of the down swing comes from positive big muscle action. Another important property of muscles is that they can only pull, not push. In general, big muscles work at their greatest efficiency and give their greatest power when working comparatively slowly; whereas small muscles give their peak performance when moving faster.

Programming the Swing

Information is passed to the brain and used, together with memories stored from the results of previous experience, to come to a decision. This decision is coded in the form of nervous impulses and passed to the appropriate muscles that subconsciously carry out the tasks required of them.

An Experiment in Reaction Time A golfer hits drives into a net in a room from which all daylight has been excluded and which is lit by a single artificial light. The golfer goes on hitting shot after shot and as a measure of how good each shot is, the speed of the ball and the point on the clubface, where contact is made, are recorded.

During some swings, however, the light is switched off. When it is switched off the room is instantly plunged into darkness. The golfer knows this is going to happen sometimes but doesn't know when. The golfer is instructed that whenever the light is switched off to do whatever the golfer can to stop the swing; or, if unable to, then to at least change the swing by slowing down, by swinging over the top of the ball, or by mis-hitting it.

The object of the experiment is to find out at what stage the golfer totally committed to his shot and quite unable to alter it in any way. The light is switch off at different points in the swing.

Where would you say the point of no return is? When the club head is a foot from the ball? Or two feet? Or halfway through the downswing? In fact, that point of no return or commitment point is much earlier than any of these. Of all the many golfers tested, when the lights went out, not one golfer could alter their stroke in any way after a point just barely into the downswing. Yet, nearly all could actually stop the shot if the light went out during the backswing.

What this implies is that once any of us has fairly begun the down swing, we can't correct or alter it in any way. Tiger Woods is one exception to this.

That insight may surprise most golfers, but it didn't surprise the scientists conducting the test. Why not? Because the time the down swing takes (0.2 to 0.25) is just about the minimum time required for the brain to perceive external signals, to give orders for the appropriate action, and for the muscles concerned to do something about it.

Correcting an Error (Maybe Only on the Backswing)

Should a golfer feel they have gone wrong at any stage after their downswing has started? No, there is little the golfer can do about it. This is not to say that a shot that starts wrongly cannot be saved; but, to be saved, it must have gone wrong, and the news of this must have been passed to the brain earlier, sometime during the backswing. The golfer may not know this. He or she may well imagine that the whole correction process occurred in the downswing; but this is an illusion. The lights-out experiment demonstrated this quite clearly. The golfers tested were asked to say when they thought the light had been switched off; and, without exception, they said it had gone out later than it actually did. For example, if the light went out at the beginning of the downswing, most thought it went out at about impact.

Clicking cameras and overhanging branches...

Players often complain that a photographer distracted their concentration and spoiled their shot by taking a picture during the player's downswing. Well, in those terms, it probably couldn't happen. According to this experiment, any click during the downswing could not possibly affect the shot and would probably not even register in the player's mind until the ball had gone. However, if the camera clicked during the backswing, then the player might be aware of it in time for it to upset his concentration; and he might imagine he heard it happen during the backswing. Something readers may be familiar with—if you are playing from under a tree and you are aware of the possibility of hitting a branch near the top of your backswing, it is relatively easy, should you actually hit the branch, to stop your swing and try again. However, if you haven't noticed the branch, or if the possibility of hitting it has not occurred to you, you will find it difficult or impossible to stop.

The whole swing is programmed in advance.

The brain programs the whole series of events in the golf swing advance. It sends all-necessary instructions to the muscles before the movement actually starts. Once the operation is under way it is very difficult (and after a certain stage, impossible) to break into the system and alter it. And this, of course, is just what getting set up, waiting for the right moment to swing is all about. The golfer must marshal all his thoughts before swinging; and to do this probably any golfer needs to have one positive thought in their mind about what they are going to do during the swing.

A few checks before the swing; only one during it.

It is not really possible to think of more than one or two things in any single swing -which is why beginners find it so difficult to learn, particularly if given too much instruction at once. The first movement of the backswing, or the way you feel it, is also something that you can take time to prepare for. All golfers, good or bad, should take advantage of the time available to get these things right. In competition some positive thought should be in the player's mind for every shot, if only to block out negative ones. These positive thoughts can be almost anything. Interpreted literally, they may even be quite nonsensical. Yet they may make very good sense, in so far as their object is to achieve some real practical effect by getting the player to aim at a feeling of something imaginary. *The player must have his or her key thought absolutely clear in their mind before beginning the swing.*

Building up the beginner's program.

What we have been saying is that before every shot the player has in mind what sort of stroke needs to be played, the player takes up his or her position to hit the ball, and then it is the subconscious programmed sequence of the swing that goes to the muscles. No conscious thought is needed.

Of course, the novice has not yet developed a subconscious program to switch on, and their challenge is to build a personalized subconscious program—to learn the golf swing. When budding golfers starts to learn, they often become aware of many separate feelings from various parts of their body. But gradually, after repeating the moves of the backswing, these new golfers become less aware of individual parts of the body and begin to gain a much more general impression of the whole movement. Once the size of this movement has been increased to include the downswing and again over a period, the swing begins to feel like a unified movement. Once a new golfer has become reasonably competent, he or she must guard against giving too much consideration to movements of isolated parts of the body and guard against giving too little consideration to the continuity and rhythm of the movement as a whole. For this reason, watching a professional tournament often helps golfers of all abilities. It isn't that you need look for particular technical points on the grip, the stance or anything else, but that a general sense of timing and flow rub off on to your own swing.

Some of the following information comes from the book, *Secrets To Success in Sports and Play*, by researcher Marianne Torbert (Ph.D., Temple University, Pennsylvania). Her information is invaluable, and she should be thanked by all for her efforts to improve the way we play sports. I am sorry to report this wonderful book is out of print and hopeful that it will become available in the future.

Frequently, participants as well as some coaches really have no idea about why things happen. There are countless *how-to* books that contain misconceptions based upon either folklore of sports or the unsubstantiated opinions of popular sports figures. An understanding of the mechanics of skilled human movements requires a sound insight into the concepts of Newtonian Physics and some familiarity with anatomical structure of the body.

The understanding and application of mechanical principles can be transferred from one activity to another, whether it is little league, varsity athletics or weekend golf. Trying to understand the partnership between the physical and the mental aspects is a very real challenge.

Balance

Balance is the foundation from which we initiate all movement. We cannot effectively develop force nor can we hope for accuracy, consistency or coordination without good balance and straight joints.

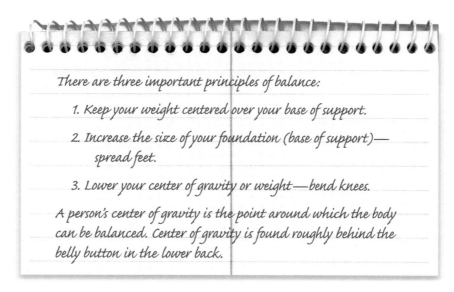

There are three important principles of balance:

1. Keep your weight centered over your base of support.

2. Increase the size of your foundation (base of support)—spread feet.

3. Lower your center of gravity or weight—bend knees.

A person's center of gravity is the point around which the body can be balanced. Center of gravity is found roughly behind the belly button in the lower back.

When the center of gravity moves nearer or beyond the outer border of the base of support instability occurs and a loss of balance starts. When losing our balance, we tend to start moving somewhat rapidly and without any conscious effort, since the pull of gravity adds to the loss of balance and our ability to create force (causing quick starts or change of direction).

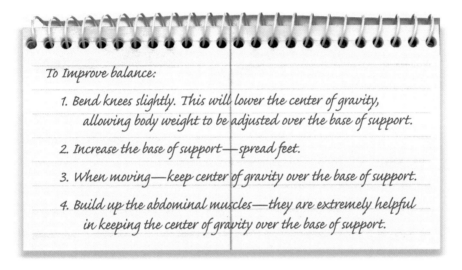

To Improve balance:

1. Bend knees slightly. This will lower the center of gravity, allowing body weight to be adjusted over the base of support.

2. Increase the base of support—spread feet.

3. When moving—keep center of gravity over the base of support.

4. Build up the abdominal muscles—they are extremely helpful in keeping the center of gravity over the base of support.

Force Buildup Requires Time and Distance

Some participants reduce the time and distance over which force is developed, believing that rushing will contribute to maximum force development. The confusion lies between getting the action done quickly or forcefully. This misconception normally fades with experience. If the act is rushed it could substantially reduce the development of force. The time and distance over which force develops can be increased by a weight transfer, opposition, lengthening the lever, and enlarging the swing arc. The elimination of any of the above reduces force development. Extraneous Movements may reduce or inhibit force production. Any movement that does not contribute directly to the movement's objective is wasteful and may even require compensating efforts to counteract its effect.

One of the goals of training should be to reduce or eliminate any unnecessary movements. Noncontributing tension will retard the build up of force and is counterproductive. Reciprocal innervations is a process by which dual messages stimulate specific muscles to contract while the opposing muscle group receives a message to relax. This allows contraction to occur without resistance. Often the beginner or one who has great desire to succeed develops a residual non-productive tension in the muscles that need to be relaxed. This excess tension inhibits the freedom and flow of movement. It helps to be aware of the effect of tension. You can learn to relax more. You can see even the highly skilled attempting to reduce their tension level. Practice swings, stretching, or a shake out of the body are all helpful. A good follow through insures maximum velocity and force at the point of impact. The complete and extended follow through assures that the slowing down process will not be initiated too early during the final part of the action phase. This means maximum velocity is still available at impact, release, or other time of need.

Opposition of the upper and lower body makes it possible to have

- Time and distance of motion
- Total muscle involvement
- Full stretch of the trunk
- Better Balance

An object will be accelerated in the direction of force applied at impact. If the direction of impact force is a scoop or chop the resulting path of the object will be different than if the direction of impact was level. In striking a ball, hopefully, the force is applied directly through the center of gravity of the object. The final weight transfer continues over a bent forward knee into the follow through. This allows for a gradual and smooth absorption of force. The bent knee also aids in keeping the center of gravity low and over the base of support thus avoiding a loss of balance that could negatively affect consistency and accuracy. The forward leg is straight at the finish of the swing.

Force Development

Force normally originates from the body's center of gravity and it then flows outward toward the end of the involved extremity. For force to develop, some portion of the body must be stabilized. This stabilized part acts as a brace against which the moving parts can push or pull and also prevents the absorption of force that would occur if there were no stabilization.

The role that stabilizers play in force production has been neglected or overlooked by many less experienced participants. For instance, many golfers are not aware of the role abdominal muscles play in the distance of their drive. Good abdominal development is necessary for several important mechanical functions:

1. Balance can be controlled better if the area in which the center of gravity is found can be held firmly.
2. The rotation of the trunk is, in part, carried out by the abdominal muscles. These muscles help to hold the pelvis, allowing the trunk movements to occur.
3. All forceful moves of the legs are dependent upon a stable pelvic foundation against which to move.
4. Forceful movement of the upper limbs originate in the pelvic region of the trunk, requiring a stabilization of the pelvic area.

The abdominal muscles stabilize the hips and create the anchor point around which the swing and weight transfer take place (anchor point or center of gravity). The abdominals play a similar role in other sports.

Flat Spot

A proper weight transfer can contribute substantially to force build up. This shift of weight also assists in timing and accuracy since transferring the body weight from the back foot to the forward foot allows for a flattening of the swinging arc. Without a proper weight transfer, the swings arc tends to be too much of a circle.

A proper weight transfer allows for the swings arc to have what is called a very small flat spot.

The flat spot occurs because your swing arc will take your center of gravity as its center. As you shift weight, the center of gravity also shifts. So you make one arc from your initial center of gravity and end up swinging around a second center of gravity position. These two arcs overlap, creating a single longer arc with a flat spot caused by the shift of weight and changing the center of gravity.

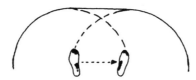

The center of gravity is moved slightly back and forth in a sound swing, not up and down. This center of gravity also never approaches the outer boarder of the base of support.

This flat spot allows the highly skilled players to hit, release or expand later in the flattened arc pattern, increasing the time and distance over which force can be developed before contact. The flat spot can also help beginners whose timing may be less than perfect.

Part IV

Feel versus *How-to*

I said we were going to talk about *feel*. What and how you—personally—feel as you play is what I am referring to. Some books have been showing the *how-to* of golf, but they are not communicating what it feels like to play good golf. The written word is digested mentally and pictures in a book are digested visually. But we play golf physically.

Low-handicap and professional golfers play the game by feel or touch. Those players can remember the feel of a good golf swing and have taught themselves to repeat that feel or touch each time they swing. You have heard it referred to as muscle memory. *Muscle memory is feel*; it is not memorizing *how-to* direction.

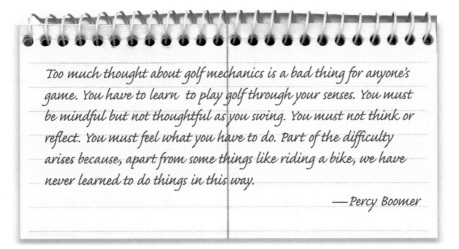

Too much thought about golf mechanics is a bad thing for anyone's game. You have to learn to play golf through your senses. You must be mindful but not thoughtful as you swing. You must not think or reflect. You must feel what you have to do. Part of the difficulty arises because, apart from some things like riding a bike, we have never learned to do things in this way.

— Percy Boomer

We have heard good golfers say they do not think about the swing when playing. They truly do not. They are playing subconsciously—by feel. Lots of things we do in our everyday life we do subconsciously by feel or muscle memory. We do most things without thinking about how to do them. You cannot think about *how-to* and get your swing to be repetitive. But you can try to make your swing feel the same way all the time. Remember what the swing feels like and repeat that feel instead of taking a *how-to* approach.

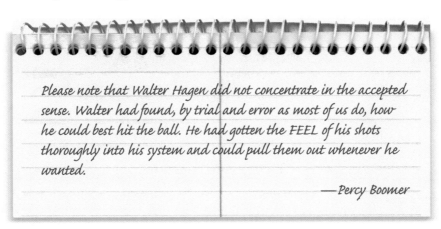

Please note that Walter Hagen did not concentrate in the accepted sense. Walter had found, by trial and error as most of us do, how he could best hit the ball. He had gotten the FEEL of his shots thoroughly into his system and could pull them out whenever he wanted.

— Percy Boomer

The *what-to-do* in golf is very important, but only to a point. You must start to feel what the what-to-do feels like if you are going to repeat your swing. When you hit a shot, good or poor, the individual characteristics of what you feel should be recognized. If your goal is to have a golf swing that can respond to what has been called prerecorded muscle memory, please accept that you should not be trying to memorize *how-to* directions.

True progress—to play better golf with consistency—comes when the *what-to-do* in golf is joined with feel. When the feel of the swing starts to become more important, than the *how-to* directions, you have started to achieve progress that lasts.

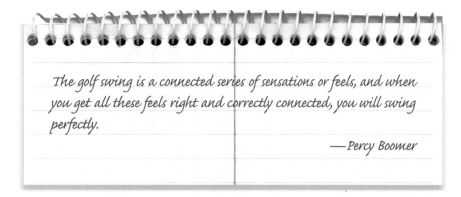

The golf swing is a connected series of sensations or feels, and when you get all these feels right and correctly connected, you will swing perfectly.

—Percy Boomer

We have all seen athletes go through some sort of pre-performance routine. Then, when motion is about to start, they walk away and start all over. The reason they walked away was they did not FEEL right. They are very good at what they do, but they have to feel it before they can do it. Baseball players are always starting over after they appear to be set. All of us in our everyday life, after we start to be good at one thing or another, will say, "I have the feel of it (or the muscle memory) to do it again." We have all said it. We have all done it. So how do you think you did it? You remember what it feels like, and then repeat the feel, not the *how-to* directions. *When a good golfer is standing over a shot, he or she is trying to repeat the feel of the address position, not thinking thoughts of do this or do that.* When the swing starts, he or she is trying to feel the movement. As the swing moves to the top of the back swing, he or she feels some thing that seems to be a signal that it is time to go down.

Expert golfers, both professional and amateur, have filled out questionnaires on what they feel when playing (not how they play). We are going to use these answers to help define what you are feeling in your golf game and give you new tools to make progress.

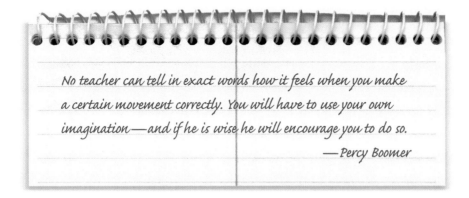

> *No teacher can tell in exact words how it feels when you make a certain movement correctly. You will have to use your own imagination—and if he is wise he will encourage you to do so.*
>
> —Percy Boomer

Golf attracts new players every day because it looks like fun and not too hard to play. Also, any golfer who has a nice game will tell you that golf is not all that hard. The truth is, if you follow a few fundamentals and practice, things can fall into place for your game. When you read what good players feel when playing, you will have another tool to learn with.

Because no two golfers would feel the swing the same way, this section may confuse you. But if you have never paid attention to the feel of your swing, it's time you did. It is a key that could help you to have a consistent swing. It is the brain's right hemisphere at work! Listed on the following pages are statements from some leading golfers about feel, followed by answers to the questionnaire. Use the answers, not as guidelines to what you should be feeling, but as tools to help you in defining your own feel.

Bobby Jones: "The primary aim in teaching must be to communicate to the golfer the feel of making a proper golf stroke."

Ben Hogan: "I am an advocate of the kind of teaching which stresses the exact nature and feel of the movements a player makes to achieve the results he wants."

Arnold Palmer: "The swing is largely a matter of feel."

Gary Player: "There is a definite 'feeling,' and this feeling is to be *developed and looked for.*"

Jack Nicklaus: "I'll try to 'feel' the shot, *generally, rather than specifically,* then swing before I lose the feel."

Johnny Miller: "The *golf swing* is built largely on *muscle memory.*"

Ben Hogan: "The more a golfer can trust his swing to muscle memory (feel), the more attention he can then turn to managing his game."

Jack Nicklaus: "Another point about swing '*symmetry.*' Get it out of your head. You should feel you are making the same basic swing with every dub."

Ben Hogan: "A good golfer acquires feel and rhythm through practice."

Jack Nicklaus: "In practice I am developing *feel.*"

Jack Nicklaus: "To me, once your mechanics are reasonably sound, *feel* becomes the *critical factor.*"

Survey

TP =Teaching Professional • LT = Ladies' Tour • MT =Men's Tour

Do You Have Any Thoughts about Feel?

TP   Feel is an important part of the game. But it is only developed through the constant practice of the fundamentals.

LT   I believe it can be taught and that it varies from day to day—some days you can feel certain keys better; other days may have to be more mechanical.

LT   The only way by which one should strive to play the game. By feeling the movements—good or bat—one can then correct or maintain them. Playing the game by feel, one allows the subconscious mind to do its job of swinging the club. Practicing by feel is the most effective way the conscious mind will tell (teach) the subconscious proper swing positions. Proper visualization is essential as well and works to promote proper feel.

LT   It is the one thing that takes the golfer from the good ranks to the professional or great player ranks. This is because not all shots are meant to be full shots. If you hit a five iron 155 yards—what do you do if you have 148–158 yards to the pin? OR if you have a 35-foot putt or slow Bermuda Greens versus fast bent grass?

MT   Yes, definitely—you must feel the shot in advance pinpointing your feel at contact and working toward a balanced firm finish!

MT   I believe golf is all feel, that's why good players can lay off for months and come right back to winning forms.

MT   Feel should be more a part of instruction than it currently is—it is what separates the players from the mechanical players.

MT   I think it is the most important part of advancing in teaching a pupil. Once he can get some feeling of what he is trying to do then you are on your way to helping and improving him—*no feel*—*no player*—there are a lot of bad swingers, but great players are "great" because they have a feeling of club—muscles, rhythm, etc. I have never met or talked to good players who are not always talking and using the word feel in describing or *explaining* types of shots and swings.

LT   To me feel is the key to the whole game:

(1) Helps tempo;
(2) Is the key for hitting the shot pin high.

Hitting the shot on line every time is exceptional, but the player hitting the shot pin high every time to me play with topic, feel. So, the player, especially the beginner and the high handicapper, should work harder on judging how far the shot is, they would score better if they knew their distances better. Great players that play with feel for distance: Boros, Trevino, Casper, Littler, Bolt. They don't have to walk off the distance—they take a look and hit. Maybe this is a gift that we don't all have. One thing they do have in common is feel.

In Terms of Feel, What Does Your Address Feel Like?

TP   Comfortable, with as much tension taken out of the right side as possible.

TP   I feel an upward feeling through my body but a hanging feeling from the shoulders.

TP   More weight on the right side enables me to pull my left knee behind the ball.

TP   Comfortable—usually soft, alert, getting a preliminary feel of what the ball will do!

TP   I try to feel as upright as possible. Not stiff but tall. My knees flexed but not locked.

TP   I feel I am well balanced and there isn't any tension in my body.

LT   Feels like my left side is a little higher—kind of like I'm ready to wind up from the feet *up*!

LT   (1) Depending upon shot being played;
(2) My weight distribution is what I feel more to the left on shorter shots, etc.

LT   Feel right side (shoulder-hip-arm) hangs from my left. 75% of my weight is on my right foot—ball of foot to heel.

LT   My best address position—balance; muscle set; steadiness and solidity over ball; comfortable; effortless; no excess motion; fluidity possible in preparing for swing.

LT   I feel parallel with shoulders, hips, feet and line of flight. I feel club face square to imaginary line of flight in my mind.

LT   After a basic address position is established for myself through practice and observation, I just try to repeat this by repetition and comfort is the most important feel.

MT   Comfortable, on balance with most of weight on left side.

MT   My address feeling is of proper width of feet, with a good solid distribution of weight from heel to toes, and a continuous feeling of movement and rhythm-shifting.

MT   Relaxed, but taut left side.

MT   Comfortable and not contrived—muscles ready to respond.

MT   Shoulders and hips just left of target—feet at target or just right—weight on inside of feet (balls of feet)—legs braced against each other.

MT   My arms are hanging naturally. I feel as if I have a little more weight on the inside of my right foot. My knees are slightly flexed and a slight bend from the waist. My shoulders feel wide, not hunched.

MT   I feel comfortable or relaxed in my legs, arms hang freely approximately six to nine inches away from stomach. Stance is slightly open. Legs are slightly flexed.

MT   At address, I feel very relaxed in the bottom of my feet—I'm ready to spring straight up. I feel like a quarterback in position behind a center.

MT   I stand as close to the ball as possible. I feel solid in my thighs and lower back because of sit down type position.

What Do You Feel When You Hold the Club?

TP   I feel the club is not too light or heavy for me. My grip is correct and I am not holding the club too tight.

TP   The pressure feels light but the left hand feels in control.

TP   Unity in the two hands and a feel for the overall club.

TP   Get your arms feeling really light so that you can feel club head.

LT   Hands felt to work like a unit—firm pressure from both hands—yet a softness to the touch.

LT   Just try to maintain enough pressure to grip the club with control.

LT   (1) Size of grip;
      (2) Stiffness of shaft;
      (3) Head weight.

LT   Try to make my hands comfortable—have even grip pressure at all points of contact between grip of club and hands.

LT   Different things—more than one gets good results. Varying feelings of: calmness hands telling me direction of swing; relaxation but not necessarily looseness; sometimes awkwardness if forcing hands to make a change; awareness of weight of club and balance of club; familiarity of a club I've seen many times.

MT   Club head mostly. Try to feel the entire club, predominantly the club head.

MT   Equal Pressure in both hands. Both hands feel as one—firmness without tension.

MT   Firmness up left arm and in last three fingers of left hand—feel of the leather on the grip in the fingers of my right hand.

MT   That the club must feel in its proper position in my hands—more in palm and(muscle-pad) feeling of my left hand with definite finger feeling in the right hand. *Stress on pressure points—of my grip.*

MT   Get hands to feel as one unit—helps to get left thumb directly down middle of grip.

MT   I feel greater grip pressure in my left hand, preferably in the last three fingers. My right side is a bit more passive than the left.

MT   Depends on the shot!
      (1) Sometimes a light "neutral" feeling in the hands (both hands as one);
      (2) Sometimes a lock with left hand; and right hand light;
      (3) Sometimes a loose fidgety feel.

MT   I feel pressure in the last three fingers of my left hand and two middle fingers on my right. This pressure is only firm enough to hold on to the club.

MT   I feel the handle then I lift the head a little off the ground so I can feel the head.

MT   Don't know.

What Do You Feel During Backswing?

TP   A windup of the left side around the trunk of the body.

TP   A gradual feeling of increasing tightness as the back swing progresses. Less tightness for a short shot. Mostly tension not grip tension.

TP   I feel my body coil up behind the ball and my left arm feels completely straight.

TP   A coiling of the left side against the right leg. I feel my whole back swing as a movement of my left shoulder under my chin.

TP   My body coiling—but only for a split second.

LT   I feel my feet more during my swing than anything else—my left foot rolls inward as the club starts away from the ball—and the back swing just winds up.

LT   A smoothness and coiling.

LT   (1) Shoulder turn;
(2) A set-position at the top—I feel something with my wrists at
    the top.

LT   Very little. It's mental for me. I have a picture in my mind of what I want to do and when I feel I am in the proper position I automatically just let my swing happen.

LT   I feel a coiling of my whole body without knowing where the club is.

MT   Good long left arm extension; winding of the lower back muscles.

MT   Shoulders moving club away—coiling—attempting to feel club behind me.

MT   Upper torso turning with hands going up staying under the club.

MT   Moving into it smoothly from my address position set-up with concentration of turning and staying over the ball.

MT   I try to have no feel except left side domination, as slow as possible. I also try to avoid any sudden moves at top.

MT   (1) When swinging well—an absence of any tension;
(2) When not swinging well—an awareness of tension to be consciously overcome!

MT   I am feeling target-conscious. That must come to mind.

MT   Whole left side coils against braced right side.

MT I feel my arms swing back as a result of a good shoulder turn. As my shoulders turn, my hips turn until I feel my left knee behind the ball. I like to feel as if I pause at the top.

MT Turning right hip level.

MT I try to feel tempo or smoothness. I do not want to be quick, extension back away from the ball.

MT Patience, and I feel strength gathering in my body during the back swing.

MT I have the feeling of smoothness, acceleration and balance.

What Do You Feel During Downswing?

TP I feel my lower body spins very fast and my hands whip through.

TP A release of the tightness by starting with my legs first.

TP I feel my legs driving at the ball in a flexed position and my left arm feels like it returns to the ball in a straight rigid position.

TP An unwinding of the muscles that were coiled on the back swing.

LT I feel *power*, being generated, ever increasing, through and past the hitting area.

LT I feel a tremendous burst of energy and a throwing action—all in a super short moment.

LT I feel a thrust across my right foot as my left arm starts back down—I feel rhythm from my feet up my legs.

LT I feel the line of flight and a smooth unwinding, yet much accelerated from the back swing. Solid contact.

LT I feel that I just reverse the series of the back swing with the feeling that I am applying more pull on the forward swing than on the take away.

LT Total move to finish; completion of visual image of hit at ball; balance in motion; feel things relative to mechanical things I'm working on; in good swings effortlessness.

MT Lower left leading with free arm swing—head stays in position.

MT Weight return to left side, hands ahead of club using club as late as possible and a rotation of the body after contact.

MT   The continuation of the total swing that got you to the top of the back swing, and now feeling like coming into the forward swing by rocking or shifting laterally to my left side.

MT   Legs reverse swing, right hip fires through ball toward target.

MT   I feel I initiate the forward swing by replanting the left heel and pulling with my left side. Sometimes I feel as if I push off the inside of my right foot.

MT   Staying behind the ball. The smooth shifting of the body to the left side.

MT   Patience and quietness in my change of direction—then I feel the impulse of energy I built in my back swing release.

MT   All thoughts are at the flag, it's hard to feel anything but the club going through.

MT   I try to feel a strong drive with knees and legs to move to left side before impact. Left hip to clear.

MT   Acceleration and release of the club down the target line.

Do You Have Any Special Feeling at the End of Your Swing?

TP   I have a feeling of being stretched down the line of the shot with the club ending up in a high position to the left of the line.

TP   A spent feeling at the end of my swing.

TP   That the feeling of the swing has been completed with very little effort.

TP   No, other than a feeling of good balance on the shots where everything occurred in the proper sequence.

TP   I like to have an around type of feeling with the weight on the left side.

TP   That my body still occupies the same place at the finish that it did at the start and my left knee is still flexed.

LT   I feel totally released across and through to the left side with my weight rolled over on outside of left foot slightly.

LT   Balance. A rocking back on right side once shot is under way. Relaxation.

LT   Relaxation still with firm grip on club in a balanced mode.

LT   If it has been a good swing, I feel relaxed except—I fight to keep my hands or arms from folding over my shoulder—never allow right hip or right shoulder to rise above left hip or shoulder—when this position feels uncomfortable—I walk away.

LT   Balance; good swing feels like nothing happened.

MT   Not really.

MT   Balance and freedom.

MT   Not so much—think more of hitting area and releasing there! End of swing doesn't matter, it is over with by then.

MT   Balanced—could pick up right foot—90% weight on left leg.

MT   I like to feel as if I've really extended through the shot and finish high.

MT   Reaching for the sky.

MT   Balance and hands high.

MT   (1) When swinging well—balance and controlled force;
(2) When not swinging well—anticipation and anxiety.

MT   I feel completely unwound. Just to finish in as balanced a position as possible.

MT   I feel I've completed my swing best when my head is brought up by the momentum of the follow through. ONLY never forcing myself to watch the ball go down the fairway.

MT   I like to feel balanced. If the shot is good I feel good. If the shot is bad I feel bad.

MT   Relaxation.

During the Swing, Is Your Head Part of the Total Feel, or Is There a Special Feel for the Head?

TP   I feel as though my head is the center of the swing and everything revolves around it.

TP   My head is stationary—my body is detached and separate from head.

TP   Your head is separate from the rest of your body. You should feel it is on a pedestal.

TP   Part of the total, although the central part.

TP   I don't think much about the head, however, I must admit I did a lot in practice.

LT   My head feels like it stays behind the ball throughout my swing, but other than that I don't think about it or feel it.

LT   Part of total feel. It feels free to move (rotate). Relaxed neck muscles.

LT   It does its own thing as far as allowing the body to swing around itself and remain behind the ball until impact.

LT   No, has nothing to do with my feel during the swing.

LT   On the downswing of a good swing I feel my head stays way behind the ball—actually my main two thoughts are head behind legs through.

LT   Head would be part of feel if working on position; however, I associate more visual images to my head.

MT   Try not to move head by keeping eyes focused on ball through impact then head goes with club head.

MT   I like it to feel relaxed in neck and natural—but try to keep it as still as I can.

MT   Part of the total feel, I try to keep it up on the back swing.

MT   Part of the total feel.

MT   Head attached to spine—spine moves in swing so the head must move too.

MT   During impact I feel like my head is behind the ball. I try to keep it as steady as possible in my total swing.

MT   Rock steady.

MT   The head should stay as I can keep it. The head can move off the ball and back on to the ball.

MT   I try to keep my head high and feel the rest of my body working beneath my head.

MT   Sometimes the head is used as the hub! Most times it follows the action of the swing naturally. Playing well there is almost no strain in the neck.

Do You Feel Any Different When Playing Short Game Shots?

TP I only feel a shorter distance that the club travels.

TP More weight on left side during address.

TP Yes, I feel the shot with my hands.

TP The overall feel is lighter and slower.

TP I just try to have control of the club early in the swing.

TP No, it's just a mini-swing. Less wrist action because the swing doesn't progress as far.

LT I don't feel as much in my feet—but feel the distance for 50—70 yard shots more with my left arm and shoulder—feel my hands more on shorter shots—maneuver the club head with hands.

LT Firmer—more definite stroking motion. My whole feeling is concentrated on line of shot.

LT Yes—the short shots are feel in that there is no set swing for easy shots—you and your mind with reference to your reflexes determine how far you move the ball. You have to feel the distance rather than the swing.

LT Yes, in my set up I feel a change of weight distribution—everything else the same.

LT Yes—each situation presents different requirements—after deciding what shot is called for I rely on memory of the feel I had of a successful shot that was similar to the one called for. Only constant is feel of head staying still.

LT Yes. Same qualities in a different form.

MT No—short swing is just a segment of long swing.

MT Very definitely! Like a softer but firm grip and even change my grip on shorter shots at times because I want a special feel for special shots.

MT Yes, my arms "feel" softer. I relax my grip when playing shots that require a lot of feel.

MT Yes—total looseness.

MT I try to exaggerate tempo. Keep it slow and accelerate the club through impact.

MT I feel less energy build on my back swing.

MT Softer; quieter—feelings are mostly mental and I make a big effort to encourage positive feelings.

MT I try to feel the distance. I grip lighter to aid my touch.

MT More precise, more stable, more solid, more left side oriented.

MT The shorter the shot—the less motion used—feel is basically same.

Some Closing Thoughts

We all can improve, but first it will be helpful to understand:

A. The golf swing is a motor skill and should be learned with the same approach as other motor skills. This means beginning with the simplest actions and then moving step-by-step to the more intricate motions.

B. A student should never go on to the next step until they have made progress with the initial fundamentals. Too often, students move along before they are really ready, never fully grasping the concept, and the learning experience is fragmented or impaired. They have not mentally graduated to the next step. Our body will improve with work and properly supervised practice with a specific goal in mind.

C. The mind relates best to images, movements, results, and feedback, not words. A mental image precedes every physical action that we perform.

In all skill learning, there is a short period of ***intellectual*** or ***analytical*** learning. It is during this period that a student learns the fundamentals. This is followed by the ***conceptual stage*** where the student learns the function of the body and the golf club. The intellectual and conceptual stages liberate the ***creative elements*** of a student, allowing them to play golf. To play good golf, we need to use our imagination and creativity to gain the know-how or operational intelligence of playing golf.

Summary

- Your ability to make progress in golf will depend, for the most part, on the amount of time and effort you invest in the many challenges the game presents.

- You also must believe that it is how we mentally visualize the shot and swing before-hand, that can make a real difference in the quality of your game.

- Most, if not all, power in sports is a direct result of a rotation of weight, and golf is no exception.

- We would like all of our swings to have rotational force, and when *the Inside is moving the Outside* rotational force will be present.

- Please start to remember the feel of your good swings, and try to repeat that feel the next time you swing. Do not think about the ball, or swing theories.

- Stay smooth when you play golf. Take your time, relax and play in the state of grace. Your golf swing does not have to be fast or hard to have power.

- Have patience when your golf is not what you would like it to be. Your game will come and go, this is the nature of golf. Have patience when your progress seems slow.

- Find yourself a good golf instructor that you can trust and work with him/her on a regular basis.

- Last, I hope you find our ideas and point of view helpful, and that they lead to more enjoyment when playing this game we all love.

To Be Continued...

We never know what the future holds, especially when it comes to what may be possible.

I know I will keep looking.

Best of luck pursuing your goals.

—Michael

*Suggested Reading**

Drawing on the Right Side of the Brain
by Betty Edwards

Inner Game of Golf
by Tim Gallow

Bobby Jones on Golf
by Bobby Jones

Golf Is My Game
by Bobby Jones

On Learning Golf
by Percy Boomer

Better Golf Without Practice
by Alex Morrison

A New Way to Better Golf
by Alex Morrison

*The Four Magic Moves
to Winning Golf*
by Joe Dante

The Venturi Analysis
by K. Venturi

The Golf Secret
by H. A. Murray

Exercise Fitness for Golf
National Golf Foundation

One Move to Better Golf
by Carl Lohren

The Full Swing
by Jack Nicklaus

The Modern Fundamentals of Golf
by Ben Hogan

Power Golf
by Ben Hogan

5 Days to Golfing Excellence
by Chuck Hogan

The Search for the Perfect Swing
by A. Cochran & John Stobbs

30 Exercises for Better Golf
by Frank W. Jobe, M.D.

Golf in the Kingdom
by Michael Murphy

Maximum Golf
by John Schlee

*from First Edition in 1984

1982

For information concerning
Michael Hebron's
Workshops/Seminars,
Clinics, or
Private Lessons
Please visit us at *www.michaelhebron.com*
Smithtown Landing Country Club
495 Landing Avenue
Smithtown, New York 11787
or call
1-800-444-0565 (toll-free)
or 1-631-979-6534
fax 1-631-979-8025

Some References (from 2007)

Smart Moves	Dr. Carla Hannford
Mindstorms	Seymore Papert
Mindfulness	Dr. Eleanor Langer
The Power of Mindful Learning	Dr. Eleanor Langer
Mastery	George Lenord
How the Mind Works	Steven Pinker
The Seat of the Soul	Gary Zukaz
Keeping Mozart in Mind	Dr. Gordon Shaw
The Secret of the Soul	Stuart Wilde
Cooperative Learning	Dana L. Grisham & Paul M. Molinell
No Quick Fix	Richard L. Allington & Sean A. Walmsley
A History of Knowledge	Charles Van Doren
How to Think Like DaVinci	Michael L. Geib
Seven Steps to Genius	Michael L. Geib
Switching On	Dr. Paul E. Dennison
Extraordinary Golf	Fred Shuemaker
Rethinking Golf	Chuck Hogan
How People Learn	National Research Council
The Absorbent Mind	Maria Montessori
The Educated Child	William J. Bennett
The Story of Stupidity	James F. Willes, Ph.D.
Magical Child	Joseph Chiliore Pearce
Leonardo—The First Scientist	Michael White
Creative Visualization	Neville Drury
The Food Revolution**	John Robbins
Myself, A Case of Mistaken Identity**	Allan Watts
Frogs Into Princes	Richard Bandler
Peak Performance: Mental Training Techniques of the World's Greatest Athletes	Charles Garfield
Reframing	Richard Bandler & John Grinder
Heart of the Mind	Connierae Andreas
Core Transformation	Connierae & Tamara Andreas
The Inner Game of Tennis	Tim Gallwey
The Sweet Spot In Time	John Jerome
The Zone	Rhea White & Michael Murphy
All I Really Need to Know, I Learned in Kindergarten (1993)	Robert Fulgham
The Dominance Factor	Dr. Carla Hannaford
Dance of the Wui Li Masters; An Overview of the New Physics	Gary Zukau
Space, Time and Beyond	Bob Tooben &Fred Alan Wolfe
Instant Report	Michael Brooks
Influencing With Rapport	Gerri Laore
Motherronge	Bill Bryson
Perfect Health	Deepak Chopra
Ageless Body, Timeless Mind	Deepak Chopra
Run Your Brain for a Change	Bandler & Andreas
Trance-Formations	Bandler & Andreas
The Continuum Concept	Jean Liedlof
Juicing for Life	Cherie Calbom & Maureen Keane
Dining in the Raw	Rita Romano
Eating For Optimum Health	Andrew Weil
Fit For Life II	Harvey & Marilyn Diamond
Reversing Heart Disease	Dr. Dean Ornish
On Education	Immanuel Kant
Inventing Better Schools	Phillip C. Schlechty
The Quality School Teacher	William Glasser, M.D.
The Great Game of Business	Jack Stack
Children Teach Children	Alan Gartner, Mary Kohler & Frank Reissman
The Double Helix of Education and the Economy	Sue F. Berryman & Thomas R. Bailey
A Brain for All Seasons	William N. Calvin
Ideas and Opinions	Albert Einstein
Teacher Manual #1	C. P. Zaner
The Quotable Teacher	Randy Howe
Golf Parent for the Future	Lynn Marriort & Pia Nilsson
The Coming Era in Science	Holcomb B. Noble
Inventing Better Schools	Phillip C. Schlechty
The Golfing Machine	Homer Kelly
Synaptic Self (How the Brain Becomes Who We Are)	Joseph LeDoux
The Life We are Given	George Leonard & Michael Murphy
Philosophy	Jay Stevenson, Ph.D.
The Key to Understanding U.S. History	Khloran, Zimmer & Jarreh
Dumbing Us Down	John Taylor Gatto
Understanding Waldorf Education	Jack Petrash
The Power of Now	Eckhart Tolle
Mapping Human History	Steve Olson
Working With Emothional Intelligence	Daniel Goleman
What Is Philosophy	Gilles DeLeuze & Felix Guattari
Leonardo, The First Scientist	Michael White
Talks to Teachers	William James
Vital Lies, Simple Truths	Daniel Goleman
The Art of Being	Erich Froman
Emotional Intelligence	Daniel Goleman
Working Knowledge	Thomas R. Bailey, Katherine L. Hughes & David Thornton Moore

The Owners Manual For the Brain — Pierce J. Howard, Ph.D.
From Conception to Birth, A Life Unfolds — Alexander Tsiaras & Barry Werth
Keeping Mozart in Mind — Gordon L. Shaw, Ph.D.
E=MC², A Biography of the World's Most Famous Equation — David Bodanis
Who Are You — Malcolm Godwin
Games — Jessie H. Bancroft
The Disciplined Mind — Howard Gardner
Teaching with The Brain In Mind — R. Brasch
How Did Sports Begin? — Alfie Kohn
What Does It Mean to Be Well Educated? — William H. Caluin
A Brief Histroy of the Mind — Stephen Jay Gould
The Book of Life — Michael S. Gazzaniga, Richard B. Ivory & George R. Mangun
Cognitive Neuroscience — Sally Shaywitz, M.D.
(The Biology of the Mind)
Overcoming Dyslexia — Mike Samuels, M.D. & Nancy Samuels
Seeing with The Mind's Eye — Susan A. Greenfield
The Human Mind Explained — Ronald Kotilak
Inside The Brain — Daniel L. Schacter
The Seven Sins of Memory — Michael J. Gelb
Discover Your Genius — Gary Marcus
The Birth of Your Mind — Dr. Haim G. Ginott
Between Parent and Child — Dr. Haim G. Ginott
The Society of the Mind — Maruin Minsky
The Unschooled Mind — Howard Gardner
In Every Kid Lurks a Tiger — Rudy Duran with Rick Lipsey
Fires In the Bathroom — Kathleen Chushman
The Discovery Of The Child — Maria Montessori
Teaching To The Brain's Natural Learning Systems — Barbara K. Given
On The Sea Of Memory — Jonathan Cott
Promoting Active Learning — Chet Meyers & Thomas B. Jones
Education For Thinking — Deanna Kuhn
The Pressured Child — Michael Thompson, Teresa Barker
Teacher Man — Frank McCourt
Becoming A "Wiz" at Brain-Based Teaching — Marilee Sprenger
Crash Course — Chris Whittle
Critical Thinking, Warm Up Activities — Sparks Publishing
Tiger's Bond Of Power — Chuck Hogan
A Different Kind Of Teacher — John Taylor Gatto
Scientific American Mind Magazine
Scientific American Magazine
American Educator (Quarterly)
Dewey on Education (1959) — Marting S. Dworkin
World Perspectives in Education (1900) — Francis Bacon

The Power of Intention (2004) — Dr. Wayne W. Dyer
Games (1909) — Jessie H. Bancroft
The Learning Gap (1992) — Harold Stevenson & James Stigler
The Abandoned Generation (1995) — William Willimon & Thomas Naylor
Control Theory in the Classroom (1986) — William Glasser M.D.
The Quality School — William Glasser M.D.
Smart Shools (1992) — David Perkins
The Learning Brain (2005) — Sarah Jayne Blackmore & Uta Frith
The Ancient Engineers (1960) — L. Sprague De Camp
Peak Learning (1991) — Ronald Gross
Why Choose this Book (2006) — Read Montague
Journey Without Goal (1981) — Chogyam Trungpa
Education for Thinking (2005) — Deanna Kuhn
What Great Teachers Do Differently (2004) — Todd Whitaker
The Book (1966) — Alan Watts
Animals in Translation (2005) — Temple Grandin & Catherine Johnson
Education and the Good Life (1926) — Bertrand Russell
Against School Reform (2002) — Peter Themes
Teaching with Fire (2003) — Sam Intrator & Megan Scribner
Dr. Montessori's Own Handbook — Maria Montessori
A Short History of Nearly Everything — Bill Bryson
The Last Days of Socrates (1954) — Translated by Hugh Tredennick
American Ideas and Education (1964) — Frederick Mayer
The Inner Game of Work (2000) — W. Timothy Gallwey
Productive Learning (2007) — Stanistaw Gtazek & Seymore Sarason
On Intelligence (2004) — Jeff Hawkins & Sandra Blakeslee
Brain Facts (2000) — Eric Jensen
Understanding How Students Learn (2006) — Karen Murphy & Patricia Alexander
Harvard Business Review on Breakthrough Thinking — Harvard Business School Press
Insights on Genius (2000) — Arthur Miller
Made to Stick (2007) — Chip & Dan Heath
History of Education (1886) — F. V. N. Painter
Thinking for a Change (1989) — John C. Maxwell
To Know as We Are Known (1993) — Parker Palmer
Higher Education Journal Thought on Action
Intelligence, A Brief History (2004) — Anna Cranciolo & Robert Sternberg
The Birth of the Mind (2004) — Gary Marcus
Fires in the Bathroom (2003) — Kathleen Cushman
John Dewey's Philosophy (1939) — Joseph Ratner
Thomas Jefferson's Corresponce and Memoir (1829) — Vols. I–IV
On the Origin of Species (1861) — Charles Darwin
Out of My Later Years (1950) — Albert Einstein

The Descent of Man (1871)	Charles Darwin
Multiple Intelligences	Howard Gardner
Discover Your Genius	Michael K. Gelb
Between Parent and Children	Dr. Haim G. Ginott
The Einstein Almanac	Alice Calaprice
The Pressured Child	Michael Thompson, Ph.D.
The Red Pencil	Theodore R. Sizer
On Intelligence	Jeff Hawkins
Enriching the Brain	Eric Jensen
Memory 101 for Educators	Marilee Sprenger
How to Teach so Students Remember	Marilee Sprenger
A History of Education (1886)	F.V.N. Painter, A.M.
The Tao of Pooh	Benjamin Hoff
Touching Peace	Thich Nhat Hanh
The Aims of Education	Alfred North Whitehead
Illusions: The Adventures of a Reluctant Messiah	Richard Bach
Enriching the Brain (2006)	Eric Jensen
Understanding Creativity (2004)	Jane Purto, Ph.D.
How to Teach So Students Remember (2005)	Marilee Sprenger
The Art and the Creation of Mind (2002)	Elliot W. Eisner
The Construction of Reality in the Child	Jean Piaget
Piaget for Teachers	Hans Furth
Toward a Theory of Instruction	Jerome Bruner
Learning to Teach, Teaching to Learn	Doug Bryan
Introduction to Piaget	P. G. Richmond
Rediscovering Hope	Richard Curwin
Fiscal Reading for Stress of Change	Paul Mort
Guiding Free Expression in Children's Art	Helen Merritt
The Origins of Intelligence in Children	Jean Piaget
The Psychology of Learning	Robert Porger & A. E. M. Seaborne
A Guide to Reading Piaget	Molly Brearley & Elizabeth Hitchfield
How to Change the Games Children Play	Don Morris
A Thinker's Journal for College Freshman	Judy Daniel
I Won't Learn from You	Herbert Kohl
The Art of Awareness	Deb Curtis & Margie Carter
The Child's Conception of the World	Jean Piaget
The Development of Play	David Cohen
Horace Mann	George Hubb
Observations	Arthur Morgan
Historical Survey of Christian Educations	S. S. Laurie
Consistency	Adolfo Critto
A Teacher Speaks	Philip Marson

The Child's Conception of the World	Jean Piaget
Piaget in the Classroom	Milton Schwebel & Jane Raph
The English Reader	Lindley Murray
Teaching as Learning	Clark Moustakas
Curriculum	Martin Levit
Experience and Education	John Dewey
The Psychology of Play	Susanna Millar
The Origins and Growth of Modern Education	Elizabeth Lawrence
A Professor's Duties	Peter Markie
Creative Power	Hughes Mearns
Education at the Crossroads	Jacques Martain
The Journey to Wisdom	Paul Olson

Perhaps you would find any of my books useful:

- *The Inside Moves the Outside—Third Edition*
- *The Art and Zen of Learning Golf—Third Edition*
- *Improving Your Golf Mind, Golf Body, Golf Swing*
- *Golf Swing Secrets … and Lies*

Or any of my DVDs.

Yale University
Department of Applied Physics

Professor Robert D. Grober

November 2004

Michael,

I very much enjoyed the last couple of days: talking with you about golf and learning.

It has always impressed me that capable golf professionals develop an intuitive understanding of classical physics (i.e. forces, inertia, momentum, rotational motion, etc.). In your case, you have moved this casual relation between golf professionals and science to the next level. One can argue the essence of physics is the art of reducing problems to their core principles by seeing past outward complexities, and then communicating these ideas to others. This is what you have done for the game of golf, both in terms of your understanding of the golf swing and the way in which you relate it to students.

I saw this reduced to practice while you worked with students at Pine Needles and at the seminar you conducted for the Professional Golf Management students at Methodist College. The simplicity with which you described and demonstrated the teaching process was extraordinarily refreshing.

All the best,

Bob

"You're not trying to work on the game, you're working on yourself." Geoff Ogilvy,
2006 US Open Champion

It is your choice – the golf swing simplified or learning the golf swing simplified….

Yale University
Department of Applied Physics

Professor Robert D. Grober

May 2007

Dear Michael,

I want to express my appreciation for the tie and effort you spent traveling to Yale to participate in my class "Physics of the Game of Golf" (ENAS 140) and for our many conversations, both during this visit and over the course of the semester, that have helped me to evolve the class syllabus.

The students and I very much enjoyed your lecture, both your insights about the game of golf and your perspective on learning. The collection of pictures you have assembled and comparing the contrasting various aspects of the golf swing and their striking similarities to motion in other sports are a unique and effective method for communicating your message. It was wonderful that you took the time to join us at the driving range after the lecture, making a closer bond with those who participated.

As you well know, I am very fond of your willingness to think "outside of the box", especially when it comes to challenging the norms as they relate to learning and the relationship between student and educator. It is a healthy message, both within the golfing community and beyond.

It is always a lot of fun learning with you.

Very Sincerely,

Bob

Hofstra University

Ed Wolfarth, EdD

Professor, Physical Education & Sports Sciences

Hempstead NY

March 2007

I recently attended one of your seminars at the Long Island Golf Expo, and as a fellow "learning facilitator", I was quite impressed. You are the first golf instructor, that I have ever heard speak, who REALLY GETS IT.

Learning and not teaching is what it's all about. You were able to put a complex motor skill into simple concepts and images that learners could grasp easily. You are the quintessential teacher.

I frequently use the analogy of learning how to walk. There are no books on walking! No gurus. And yet, people around the world seem to have learned how to walk quite efficiently. As a famous child psychologist once said, "if children could talk before they could walk, walking would be the most difficult motor sill to master."

As a teacher of motor skills at Hofstra University, I have come to the realization that the less I teach, the more they learn. Of course it's not that simplistic. Putting the emphasis on the learning process, however, is key.

Keep up the good work. I hope you get the opportunity, as I have, to train future teachers. It's a rewarding experience and others need to embrace your approach.

Sincerely,

Ed Wolfarth EdD

University of Arkansas at Little Rock

Robert R. Ulmer, Chair

Department of Speech Communication

January 2006

Dear Michael,

I really enjoyed attending your three-day golf school at Southern Pines in North Carolina. Your approach to learning golf is unique and yet consistent with the best research that I know of in instruction and learning. Your focus on the misconceptions that I had about golf, the development of my own core knowledge about the game, and the positive learning environment developed at your school made my experience a very positive one.

I thought it was interesting that each day we spent some time discussing misconceptions related to the golf swing. Our discussions regarding my perceptions about what makes the ball fly and your explanation that golf club weights something have been extremely valuable to *my experience* of the golf swing. These new insights have made a huge impact on my approach to playing golf.

After completing your golf school, I felt like I developed some sound core knowledge about how I swing the golf club. You did not give me several swing thoughts to take on the course but rather core knowledge that I can work on during my practice sessions. Keeping with this idea, I realized that effective motor skill learning is about subtraction not necessarily addition. As a college professor this was an interesting and new approach for me to consider.

One of the things I appreciated the most about your golf school was the positive, supportive learning environment that you created. Without this type of environment I believe that learning golf would be much more difficult. We tried different shots and different ways to apply force to the golf ball without judgement. As I played more and judged les I found my improvement increased dramatically. I also enjoyed myself more. I have continued this approach to this day.

Michael, thank you for your guidance and instruction. I really appreciate it. I am enjoying the game more than ever!

Sincerely,

Robert R. Ulmer

Lightning Source UK Ltd.
Milton Keynes UK
UKIC01n0619101014
239846UK00009B/58

9780962021473